You reach out and just manage to seize hold of the lip of the dark pit, but your comrade disappears into the depths with a piteous scream.

You cry out to Damontir to help you. With a warm feeling of gratitude you sense him standing over you in the darkness. Then the warmth turns to a chill as you see the flash of his teeth in a wicked smile. His booted foot crunches down on your desperately clutching fingers.

You can hold on no longer. You fall back into the void, blackness reaching towards you...

Gamebooks from Fabled Lands Publishing

by Jamie Thomson and Dave Morris:

Fabled Lands 1: The War-Torn Kingdom
Fabled Lands 2: Cities of Gold and Glory
Fabled Lands 3: Over the Blood-Dark Sea
Fabled Lands 4: The Plains of Howling Darkness
Fabled Lands 5: The Court of Hidden Faces
Fabled Lands 6: Lords of the Rising Sun

by Dave Morris:

The Temple of Flame
Castle of Lost Souls

by Oliver Johnson:

Curse of the Pharaoh
The Lord of Shadow Keep

In preparation:

by Dave Morris:

Heart of Ice
Down Among the Dead Men
Necklace of Skulls
Once Upon a Time in Arabia

by Jamie Thomson and Mark Smith:

Way of the Tiger 1: Avenger
Way of the Tiger 2: Assassin
Way of the Tiger 3: Usurper
Way of the Tiger 4: Overlord
Way of the Tiger 5: Warbringer
Way of the Tiger 6: Inferno

The Temple
of Flame

DAVE MORRIS

First published 1984 by Grafton Books

This edition published 2013 by Fabled Lands Publishing,
an imprint of Fabled Lands LLP

www.sparkfurnace.com

ISBN-13: 978-1909905047
ISBN-10: 1909905046

HOW TO USE THIS BOOK

You are the Dragon Knight of Palados, a skilled warrior, the veteran of many battles. In your yearning for constant challenge and excitement you have fought trolls, ogres, goblins, mad warlocks and many other strange and terrifying opponents. The years of adventure have honed your reflexes and fighting skill so that few men could hope to stand against you in single combat.

To determine just how good a warrior you are, you must use the dice:

- Roll two dice. Add 20 to this number and enter the total in the VIGOUR box on your Character Sheet. This score represents your strength, fitness and general will to survive. Any wounds you take during your quest are subtracted from your VIGOUR score. If it ever reaches zero you are dead.
- Roll one die. Add 3 to the number rolled and enter the total in the PSI box on your Character Sheet. The higher this score, the better you are at resisting spells cast at you and the more sensitive you are to psychic impressions.
- Roll one die, add 3 and enter the total in the AGILITY box. This score reflects how nimble you are. You will need a high AGILITY to scale walls, leap across chasms, and so on.

YOUR NAME

Personalize your adventuring persona by thinking of a heroic name. You might call yourself Lucas Orcslayer or Sir Loras of the Flowers, Lady Angela Mortis or Borlak of the Black Shield, or any other name you can think of.

CHARACTER SHEET

VIGOUR	Current score:	TREASURE
AGILITY	Current score:	
PSI	Current score:	

ITEMS

magic sword
armour
knife
flask of water
backpack

OPPONENTS

VIGOUR	*VIGOUR*
VIGOUR	*VIGOUR*
VIGOUR	*VIGOUR*

VIGOUR, AGILITY and PSI

Your VIGOUR will change constantly during the adventure — every time you are wounded, in fact. You may acquire healing potions or salves on your quest. These will restore some of the VIGOUR points you have lost owing to wounds — but unless you are told otherwise your VIGOUR score must never exceed its original value. This is your *normal* score; keep a careful note of it.

Your AGILITY and PSI are less likely to change, although this is possible. Spraining your ankle, for example, might reduce your AGILITY by 1 point. A magic helmet might increase your PSI. But, as with VIGOUR, your AGILITY and PSI will never exceed their *normal* scores unless you are specifically told otherwise.

COMBAT

During the course of your adventure, you will often come across a monster or human enemy whom you must fight. When this happens, you will be presented with an entry something like this:

123

The ogre hefts his axe and advances towards you. You have no escape route, and must fight.

OGRE   VIGOUR 10

Roll two dice:
score 2 to 5   You are hit; lose 3 VIGOUR Points
score 6 to 12   The ogre loses 3 VIGOUR Points

If you win, turn to **214**.

At the start of every combat, you should record your opponent's VIGOUR score in an empty Encounter Box, You then begin the combat by rolling two dice, and, as indicated in the entry, deducting a number of points from either your own VIGOUR score or that of your opponent. If you and your opponent still have VIGOUR scores of more than 0, you repeat this procedure for successive *combat rounds,* deducting the appropriate VIGOUR points each time, until the VIGOUR score of either you or your enemy is reduced to 0 — indicating death. Keep note of the VIGOUR scores on your Character Sheet and in the Encounter Box.

ESCAPING FROM COMBAT

In some cases you may be engaged in combat and find yourself losing. If given the option, you may FLEE from the combat. Your enemy will, however, attempt to strike a blow at your unguarded back as you turn to run. To represent this, whenever you choose to FLEE you should roll two dice and compare the total to your AGILITY score. If the dice roll *exceeds* your AGILITY then you have been hit (losing 3 VIGOUR points) as you FLEE. If the dice roll is *less than or equal to* your AGILITY score, however, you dodge your opponent's parting blow and escape without further injury.

ITEMS

You are certain to come across a number of items. Some of these may turn out to be useless — or even harmful — but sometimes even the most insignificant-looking acquisition can prove vital to your quest. You should fill in items on your Character Sheet as you acquire them and cross them off as they are discarded or used up.

You begin with several important items. These have already been filled in on your Character Sheet:

- magic sword
- armour

- · knife
- · flask of water
- · backpack

THE ADVENTURE

You are now almost ready to begin. You will start by reading the PROLOGUE, and then proceed to **1** and on to further entries according to the decisions you make.

Be warned: this adventure is not easy. You are highly unlikely to find the idol of Katak on your first attempt. Make a map as you explore the temple. If you get killed, fill in a new Character Sheet and try again, using the map you made before to guide you. It may take you several attempts, but eventually you will win through to confront your arch-enemy Damontir in a battle for the gold idol of the flame god.

And now — your adventure begins…

PROLOGUE

There were three of you in the dark, damp chamber – you, Valedor and the man known as Damontir the Mad. The mists of time disperse and seem to fly away as the scene comes sharply into focus before you again. Around you are the crumbling statues and peeling murals of that forgotten tomb. Your comrades at arms, brave knights of Palados, are stiffening corpses pierced by steel or crushed by stone somewhere in the crypts and tunnels above.

Valedor holds forth his sword and a bright lance of light illuminates a carbuncle on the face of the grotesquely carved sarcophagus. Damontir lurks mysteriously in the shadows. Suddenly there is a click and the lid of the sarcophagus swings up to reveal a bejewelled crown on the brow of the mummified corpse within. But the light from Valedor's enchanted sword has activated an ancient trap, and before you can move towards the treasure, the ground beneath you gives way and you begin to fall. You reach out and just manage to seize hold of the lip of the dark pit, but Valedor disappears into the depths with a piteous scream. You cry out to Damontir to help you. With a warm feeling of gratitude you sense him standing over you in the darkness. Then the warmth turns to a chill as you see the flash of his teeth in a wicked smile. His booted foot crunches down on your desperately clutching fingers. You can hold on no longer. You fall back into the void, blackness reaching towards you…

You come awake with a start, the pounding of your heart sounding in your ears like a jungle drumbeat. You are soaked in sweat and have to struggle to free yourself from the blanket that clings to your body. From outside comes the twittering of exotic birds and the flash of dawn sunlight off the river as your ship gently wends its way upstream. You have merely dreamt how, many years earlier, the sorcerer Damontir nearly put an end to your life – how, instead of following Valedor into the abyss, your fall was broken by a hidden ledge; how, though badly wounded, you climbed back to the tomb chamber to find the crown and Damontir gone. Silently, you repeat the vow you have made to yourself every morning since that far-off day: never to rest until you have avenged yourself upon the evil sorcerer.

The green banks of the jungle slide past you on either side. Occasionally a long, black shape launches into the water with a dull splash and drifts idly towards the ship. The sailors mutter that the crocodiles of Anku can bite a man in half. The crocodiles stare up at you with blinking inscrutability, then drift off like logs in the muddy ochre water. Brightly coloured birds screech and cavort over the treetops. The wind slackens as you pass a bend in the river. Ahead, rising straight out of the shimmering water, stands a thin spire of crystal reaching up almost a hundred metres into the azure sky. You call to the sailors to lower the sail and drop anchor. Noon approaches - the hour which the ancient texts appoint as propitious for beginning the quest. Your steward reverently fastens the buckles and clasps of your armour, for you are the Dragon Knight of Palados, greatest warrior of the known world. He is barely able to lift your gleaming broadsword, though you take it from him and swing it without effort before sliding it into your scabbard. In the white, staring faces of the sailors you read awe and a little fear. You climb down into the rowboat by the ship's side and, standing at its prow, call for your men to cast off. As the rowers stretch and grunt over their oars, you concentrate on what lies ahead: the temple of the flame god, Katak, lost for eons in the mosquito-ridden depths of the forest, obscured by vines and creepers, surrounded by impenetrable swamp. Only a mouldering libram in the archives of Achtan, capital of great Palados, revealed the hints and clues which enabled you to deduce the temple's location.

A dark shadow obscures the sun. You look up; it is only the first of the branches overhanging the river as your boat approaches the bank. According to the age-stooped librarian in Achtan, one other person had consulted the book from which you gleaned your information. And he had visited the archives just a few weeks before you. The old librarian could not, however, recall the man's face – as though a magic spell had been used to cloud his memory. You ponder this as you step nimbly from the boat. The rowers look around nervously at the rustling treetops where brilliantly hued parrots fly and monkeys crash from branch to branch. 'Watch this spot,' you tell them. 'I will signal you from here when my quest is over and I have the golden idol of Katak.'

With obvious relief, they push away from the bank and head back to midstream where the ship lies at anchor. You take a last look, then turn and make your way into the waiting jungle.

NOW TURN TO 1.

1

In the depths of the jungle, the thick canopy of foliage filters the sunlight into lush green and golden hues. You struggle onwards, slowly hacking with your knife through the heavy vines and creepers that block your progress. The ground underfoot squelches with mud that soon covers your boots. Mosquitoes and fantastically coloured dragonflies swarm all around in the murky, drenching heat. Snakes, basking in the midday warmth, hang in loose, lazy coils from the branches and hiss disinterestedly as you pass. A gentle breeze stirs the treetops and the sunbeams dropping through sudden chinks in the leaves are like a cascading shower of liquid gold. A parrot shrieks and flutters through a shaft of sunlight, almost dazzling you with the sudden blaze of scintillating colour as it does so.

Eventually the going gets easier. After a while you decide to take a rest. As you crouch down to sip a little water from your hip-flask, your gaze alights on an extraordinary tableau which is being enacted only a few paces away. A tiny red-faced spider monkey squats on a flat rock, staring with wide eyes at the swaying head of a large viper that is slowly weaving towards him. The monkey is frozen in terror, and is certain to die unless you choose to intervene. If you wish to save him by killing the snake, turn to **11**. If you decide to ignore the incident and continue on your way, turn to **18**.

2

You hastily delve into the pouch in search of any magical compound that might prove useful. You sort through the various pots and vials with little idea of their effects. Your selection of the three most promising substances is based largely on guesswork and whim, therefore. Will you try:

A blue paste?	Turn to **261**
A reddish-black powder?	Turn to **90**
A green liquid?	Turn to **121**

3

You are at the north end of an unadorned gallery strewn with blocks of broken stone. Ignoring another ebony door nearby, you begin to make your way south. Suddenly a deep groan breaks the silence and, peering through the gloom, you see what looks like a huge, roughly-hewn statue lumbering towards you. Even with your miraculous sword you will have difficulty in damaging the wrinkled slate that forms the golem's body.

GOLEM   VIGOUR 15

Roll two dice:
score 2 to 6   You are struck; lose 4 VIGOUR
score 7 to 12   The golem loses 3 VIGOUR

If you FLEE by running south past the golem, turn to **72**. If you defeat it, turn to **14**.

4

The Phoenix shrieks fiercely below as you race up the staircase. Passing the archway, you see a tunnel leading north beyond it. Damontir has left his footprints in the dust of the tunnel floor. You barely glance at the two statues at the mouth of the tunnel, or the monstrous skeleton that lies before them, as you rush through the archway to head north. Turn to **208**.

5

Your sixth sense leads you to suspect a trap of some kind. You edge carefully around the perimeter of the clearing and set off through the dense jungle once more. Turn to **80**.

6

Pulling the stopper from the bottle, you sniff tentatively at the potion inside. It is odourless. You may drink this potion at any point during your adventure (including now), except when you are engaged in combat. When you do drink it, you should turn to **101** to discover what effect it has on you, but remember to make a note of the paragraph number you are at before you do, because **101** will not redirect you to that entry. You replace the stopper and put the bottle in your backpack. In the ITEMS box on your Character Sheet you should now write: 'Blue potion (see **101** for effect)'.

If you have not yet done so, you may now take the ring (turn to **45**) or the belt (turn to **174**). If you are ready to leave this room, turn to **240**.

7

The boulder bounces on the landing, arcs over you, lands a few steps further on and thunders off into the gloom. You get up and dust yourself off. A deafening crash echoes up the staircase as the boulder reaches the bottom.

You descend the remaining steps — many of them now cracked or shattered — to the bottom.

Turn to **211**.

8

The corridor soon turns to head east and eventually brings you to a black wooden door adorned with geometric gold-lacquered patterns.

If you wish to open this door turn to **3**. If you would rather return to the last junction and take the corridor leading east from there, turn to **205**.

9

As you roll aside you can feel the heat of the energy blast passing close by you. Where you were lying a moment earlier, the floor has become a pool of molten stone. You spring to your feet, realizing that you cannot keep on evading its blasts forever. However much the idea runs contrary to your warrior instincts, you will have to try to get away.

Turn to **27**.

10

The water tastes slightly bitter — but not intolerably so, and you experience no ill effects in drinking from it. Marvelling at the extraordinary sorcery that has kept the water fresh for centuries, you ponder your next move. Will you leave now and head west (turn to **119**), or will you go over and take the drum from the statue's lap (turn to **144**)?

11

Without even rising from your crouch, you snap your arm straight. Your knife flashes as it spins once in the hot sunlight and buries itself in the viper's head. The little monkey watches you incredulously as you stride over to the twitching body of the snake and pull your knife free. His expression is so comical that you roar with laughter as you sheathe your knife. Strewn all around the monkey are the cracked shells of small nuts. Clearly he was enjoying his lunch so much that he failed to notice the viper's approach.

As you turn to leave the clearing, he grabs two tiny fistfuls of nuts and scampers after you. You had intended to head directly towards the Temple of Katak, but suddenly you feel a tug at your cloak and look down to see that the little monkey has grabbed its hem between his teeth. He is very insistent that you should take a different route on into the jungle. If you do so, turn to **57**. If you would rather shake the mischievous creature off your cloak and press on as you had intended, turn to **18**.

12

The corridor widens and then comes to a dead end. There are gilded double doors in the wall to your right. You cannot track the footprints any longer because the area in front of the doors has been swept clean of dust — but deliberately, or as the result of a fight that took place here? Since the only way onwards seems to be through the double doors, you reach out to push them open. Just then, you notice the

empty black robe of a Nightmare Guard lying in the deep shadows at the corridor's end. If you wish to go over and investigate this, turn to **296**. If you would rather go through the double doors, turn to **133**.

13

You twist away as the bolt hits, but you are not fast enough to evade it. Lose 15 VIGOUR for the searing pain as it tears through your flesh and, if you are still alive, turn to **242**.

14

Resting after the titanic battle, you notice a nacreous gleam from the broken rubble of the golem's body. You search amid the shattered planes of slate and your fingers close on a rounded object in the ruins of the creature's breast. The object you hold up to the light of your sword is a conch shell trumpet with a lightning-bolt glyph engraved upon it. Note it on your Character Sheet if you decide to take it with you. Remembering that Damontir is still ahead of you, you hurry south. Turn to **72**.

15

You race along the passage and come to a halt before a heavy ebony door. There is no other way for you to go. Glancing nervously into the darkness behind you, you lift the latch and push the door open. Turn to **3**.

16

You pause by the archway. The statues are, you now see, of two warriors reaching for their swords. They face the archway with faces set in an expression of alarm. The skeletal carcass of a long-dead gorgon lies just within the shadows of the arch. Perhaps centuries have passed since it transmuted the warriors to stone with its gaze — only to die itself, eventually. Your sword illuminates the dark outlines of a tunnel beyond the archway. There is dust on the tunnel floor — and in the dust, footprints. Damontir went this way, and you follow him. Turn to **208**.

17

You fall awkwardly on your backpack and try to kick yourself through the dosing gap. At the first touch of pressure on your chest you cease your frantic struggles, freezing in a paralysis of horror as you watch the slab descend. You are powerless to move — you cannot even cry out. You do not hear the dull crunch as floor and slab meet, for your body has been gorily severed in two between them. Your adventure ends here.

18

You have gone only a few metres further when you find yourself rapidly sinking. You have blundered into one of the tracts of quicksand which encircle the temple's hidden location. It was in this way that the ancient priests of Katak protected their sacred shrine from desecration by the likes of you! You thrash wildly, but to no avail. The fluid sands roll over you, choking off your screams. Your life and your quest end here.

19

The skullghasts gradually close in to attack. You cannot help shuddering as you feel their eyeless gaze upon you. Will you meet them with drawn sword (turn to **126**), or will you take out one of the items you have collected (turn to **273**)?

20

What item will you take from your backpack:

An ebony drum?	Turn to **59**
A witchdoctor's wand?	Turn to **255**
Powdered ruby?	Turn to **127**

If you have none of these you will have to fight — turn to **41**.

21

Did you succumb to the priest-kings' curse? If so, turn to **284**. If not, turn to **60**.

22

The corridor ends in a door with an iron ring in the shape of two entwined serpents for a handle. You turn this but at first the door will not open. However, as you put your weight against it the door suddenly gives way. You stumble through, your feet slip from under you, and you careen down a smooth slope. You come to rest, shaken but unhurt, in a shallow pit filled with bare white bones. One other door leads from the room, opposite the one you entered by. As you pick your way across the floor of the pit towards this, snapping bones underfoot, something bulky and metallic reflects the glare of your sword. With slow, stalking movements of almost hypnotic menace, a giant scorpion emerges from the pile of bones ahead of you. You cannot tell whether it is a living creature or a magically animated automaton, for the armoured segments of its body seem to be fashioned of solid gold.

You start to edge around it, but you have underestimated its speed. Its opening attack comes with unbelievable swiftness. Before you can draw back, you find one of its gleaming pincers closed around your leg and you are

swinging your sword in a desperate struggle as it draws you inexorably closer to its glistening metal jaws.

GOLD SCORPION   VIGOUR 12

Roll two dice:

score 2 to 4	You are stung; lose 4 VIGOUR
score 5 to 6	You are struck by the other pincer; lose 3 VIGOUR
score 7 to 12	The scorpion loses 3 VIGOUR

It holds you fast and you cannot FLEE. Make a note during this fight of the number of times you are stung. If you win, turn to **178**.

23

As you approach the figurine, the ground gives way under your feet. Minki reacts at once and leaps from your shoulder to safety, but you are not so fortunate. You plummet down into the concealed pit and die squirming on sharp mahogany stakes at the bottom.

24

Footprints in the dust show you that Damontir and his Nightmare Guard came this way. Before long the corridor turns sharply to the right. At the bend, a fine stiletto dagger lies gleaming on the floor. If you wish to stop and pick this up, turn to **131**. If you wish to keep walking along the tunnel, turn to **190**.

25

The effect of the magic ring is to make you no more substantial than a ghost. It gives you an uncanny feeling to see the boulder roll right *through* you. As it thunders off into the gloom below, you become solid once again and the ring corrodes away and falls from your finger, its power now used up. You listen to the boulder rumble on and finally come to rest with a deafening crash, then you descend the remaining steps to the bottom.

Turn to **211**.

26

You can feel the awful venom coursing through your body. You crouch down amid the splintered bones. If you wish to take a snakebite antidote, turn to **42**. If you don't have any such antidote, or do not wish to take it, turn to **239**.

27

Where will you run: on, to the passage in the west wall (turn to **66**), or back the way you came (turn to **169**)?

28

You walk down the steps into the pool and immerse yourself completely in the cool water. If you had more time, it would be pleasant to linger here a while and bathe properly, to wash from your tired limbs all the dust and grime and blood of the last few hours. But you cannot rid your thoughts of the evil Damontir — he must not beat you to Katak's idol.

As you emerge from the pool dripping wet, you are surprised to notice that you are not shivering. When one has been swimming — even in midsummer — one feels cold when first leaving the water, surely? But you have no time for idle reverie — will you leave now to head west (turn to **119**), or will you first take the drum from the statue's lap (turn to **179**)?

29

With the elemental's flame growing stronger second by second, the temperature in the room soars rapidly. The wearying heat begins to take its toll on you. Unless you can defeat the elemental quickly, you will succumb to heatstroke.

Roll two dice:
score 2 to 7	You are hit; lose 3 VIGOUR
score 8 to 12	The fire elemental loses 3 VIGOUR

If the fight is still going on after three more Combat Rounds, turn to **68**. If you win before then, turn to **135**. You are now to weak to FLEE.

30

Unable to use the Ring of Red Ruin at close quarters, Damontir draws his own sword — a long, wickedly sharp sliver of dark crystal set in a tarnished silver hilt.

DAMONTIR THE MAD   VIGOUR 9

Roll two dice:
score 2 to 5	You are hit and lose 3 VIGOUR
score 6 to 12	Damontir loses 3 VIGOUR

If you win, turn to **300**.

31

After walking on for some minutes you arrive at a point where the trail forks sharply to the right. You squint up through the rustling trees to where the sun hangs blazing in the cobalt sky. Unfurling your map, you estimate that the temple lies almost directly ahead of you. If you decide to head straight for your goal by chopping your way through the thick foliage, turn to **80**. If you decide to remain on the twisting path, turn to **74**.

32

Any magic that resides in the wand responds only to the witchdoctor's command. As you wave it uselessly at them, two of the grisly creatures dart closer to snap at you with their fiery jaws. Lose 4 VIGOUR. If you are still alive, you heft your sword and prepare to fight. Turn to **126**.

33

You fight back and manage to repulse the psychic attack. There is a fleeting impression of spiteful thwarted evil, and then the curse you activated dissipates and fades away. Preferring not to expose yourself to the hazard of further such curses, you proceed to the end of the hall. Turn to **288**.

34

The slabs descend to the floor, blocking the corridor behind and ahead of you. You begin to search the walls for a hidden route out of this trap. Suddenly, the steady blue glare of your magic sword flickers and dies. An instant of astonishment gives way to mounting panic as you realize that only a spell of superhuman power could rob your sword of its enchantment. In the total darkness, the hard stone floor seems to dissolve or vanish from under your feet. You reach out, but cannot find the walls — the corridor has disappeared! A red glow appears in the blackness far off, and as it approaches you know that you are drifting in a void. There is no echo when you call out, only the deadening muted gulf of infinity. And now, with terror, you begin to discern the outlines of the red glow: the eyes and gaping mouth of a gigantic face. It is the visage of Katak, looming towards you across the centuries. You have violated his temple and, falling towards his volcanic maw, you will pay the ultimate price.

35

You act quickly so that the natives have no chance to stop you. Before they realize what is happening, you lunge forward and grab the witchdoctor by the throat, choking off his monotonous chant. His scrawny hand dips into the medicine pouch at his waist.

Roll one die. A 5 or 6 means that you seize his arm before he can draw anything out of the pouch (turn to **280**), but on a 4 or less you react too slowly to stop him (turn to **83**).

36

You heave the flagstone up to reveal narrow twisting steps descending into the darkness below. You draw your sword and the magic within it creates a harsh blue light that arcs along the blade. You can see now that the steps are carpeted with dust that has accumulated through millennia. Bas-reliefs along the walls show an unconstrained relish in depicting the minutiae of flayings and blood sacrifices. With Minki chattering nervously at your heels, you walk down through air so dry and stifling that it seems to begrudge you your every breath. At the bottom of the steps, you pass through a narrow triangular archway into an antechamber with an exit in the north wall, directly opposite you, and faded tapestries covering the entire length of the wall to your right. If you wish to cross the room and leave to head north, turn to **96**. If you wish to look behind the tapestry first, turn to **221**.

37

You lift the pendant up to the light and watch the large clear gem twisting on its silver chain, causing flashes of colour to dance and shimmer within. Suddenly you feel a noxious influence taking effect on you. Roll two dice and try to score equal or less than your current PSI. If you succeed, turn to **248**. If you fail, turn to **191**.

38

The curse takes its immemorial effect on you, as dictated by incantations and rituals performed two thousand years ago. You are not sure exactly what has happened to you, only that an oppressive feeling of ill fortune now afflicts you. You proceed to the far end of the hall in a brooding and demoralized mood. Turn to **288**.

39

Flanking the western end of the chamber, where the cloak hangs, are two decorative pillars in the form of plumed serpents, their heads arched tautly up against the ceiling as if poised to strike. You step between these with some trepidation and inspect the cloak. In the mingled light of the leaping flames and the steady blue glare of your sword, the cloak is an item of breath-taking beauty. It shimmers with iridescent hues of turquoise, gold and emerald green. You cannot imagine the bird from which these splendid feathers came. Will you take the cloak (turn to **193**), or will you leave it and continue on your way (turn to **294**)?

40

The silent native warriors drive you on through the jungle until you finally reach the clearing where they have their village. More natives emerge from their crude huts of dried mud and reeds to watch as you are taken to meet the witchdoctor. This gnarled old man is inspecting several huge jars of fermenting liquor in the shade of his hut. He leaps up and scurries out as you approach. After babbling incomprehensibly to the natives who captured you, he starts to jab the air with a bone wand and chant ominously. Minki seems to have disappeared, for which you can hardly blame him. You glare at the prancing witchdoctor and then at the bristling spears of the warriors around you. The native carrying your sword is standing only a few paces away. Beyond him, you notice a pole with a macabre collection of trophies dangling from it — shrunken heads. You count more than twenty. If you intend to keep your own head from joining them, you had better do something. Will you go for the witchdoctor (turn to **35**), or try to retrieve your sword from the warrior holding it (turn to **188**)?

41

You hurl yourself aside as the first of the cadavers reaches you and swings its deadly obsidian-edged war club. In your paralysis of horror, you have lost any opportunity you might have had to FLEE.

First CADAVER	VIGOUR 9
Second CADAVER	VIGOUR 9
Third CADAVER	VIGOUR 9
Fourth CADAVER	VIGOUR 9

Roll two dice:

score 2	You lose 12 VIGOUR
score 3	You lose 9 VIGOUR
score 4 to 5	You lose 6 VIGOUR
score 6 to 8	You lose 3 VIGOUR
score 9 to 12	One of the cadavers (you decide which) loses 3 VIGOUR

If you defeat one of them, turn to **268**.

42

Unluckily, the snakebite antidote causes an adverse reaction as it mingles with the venom in your blood. Your end is quick, but by no means painless. You have failed.

43

Your Simulacrum's sword clashes on yours with a shower of brilliant sparks. In its mad, murderous grin perhaps you glimpse the darkness of your own soul.

Roll two dice:

score 2 to 6	You are hit and lose 3 VIGOUR
score 7	You hit one another and each lose 3 VIGOUR
score 8 to 12	The Simulacrum loses 3 VIGOUR

If you win, turn to **283**.

44

The track winds on for some distance and then straightens out where it passes between two rows of sapling palms which bend together overhead to form a natural arbour. The air seems less humid here, the scent of the flowers less cloying. As you walk along the arbour with the dancing patterns of sunlight and leaf-shade playing across your skin, you start to whistle a tune. Were it not for the heat and the strange jungle sounds, you could almost imagine that you were strolling through the Ornamental Gardens in Achtan.

The tune dies on your lips as you espy a dozen fierce, scarified faces peering at you through the slats of entwined foliage. The 'natural arbour' is a native trap — and you have walked straight into it! You race for the far end, but barricades are swiftly lowered into place. You are caged. Blowpipes protrude through the narrow spaces between the palms. When spear-carrying natives enter the arbour and surround you, you have no alternative but to surrender your sword and allow yourself to be herded out.

Turn to **40**.

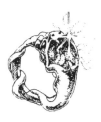

45

You slip the bronze ring on to your finger. It is a magical Ring of Intangibility. You are certain it will be of use at some point in your adventure. If you have not done so, you may now take the belt (turn to **174**) or the bottle of blue liquid (turn to **6**). If you wish to continue on your way, turn to **240**.

46

The boulder rolls over you and you are crushed to a bloody pulp by its massive weight. Perhaps, if Damontir survives to return this way, he will come upon your mangled corpse and laugh in evil glee. You have failed.

47

The phoenix feather glows brightly as you enter the column of light and suffuses you with a mystic aura. Unseen forces act to render you almost weightless. Instead of plummeting down, you drift gradually lower in the light beam. Eventually you descend right through the replica pyramid and come out into a cavern beneath it. The gravity-defying force settles you gently on the floor and you step from the beam. Turn to **224**.

48

As you rush in towards it, the creature fixes its eye upon you and stuns you with a low-power concussive blast. Lose 2 points of VIGOUR. If you are still alive, you come to only moments later to find the creature staring down at you. Its eye is an incandescent violet. It unleashes a bolt of searing red light. Throw two dice *and add 2 to the number rolled* (because dodging is more difficult when you are lying on your back). If the total is greater than your current AGILITY score, turn to **287**. If it is less than or equal to your AGILITY, turn to **9**.

49

Will you bathe in the pool (turn to **28**), or drink from it (turn to **10**)?

50

You pass a door in the left-hand wall but decide to ignore it. The corridor you are in is soon joined by another from the south. In the dust you can see three sets of footprints, obviously belonging to Damontir and his two torchbearers. You cannot tell how many of the Nightmare Guard were with him, for where these ghoulish assassins pass they leave no trace. You decide to follow the footprints west. Turn to **12**.

51

You advance warily along the path. Minki is no longer running playfully ahead, preferring to keep close to you now. Unease gnaws at you as you listen to the myriad forest noises, straining to filter from the ceaseless chatter and shrieks of bird and beast the faint sound that might betray a predator's approach. The path veers sharply to the left and you emerge into a clearing where a large wooden cage hangs from the branch of a tree. There is a young native girl within. Her wrists are bound with silver wire to a bar of the cage. She stares silently down at you, and you notice her matted hair and wild appearance. Will you cross the clearing and continue on your way (turn to **129**), or will you try to free her (turn to **271**)?

52

A rough stale odour rises from the urn as you open it. It is filled almost to the brim with black cinders. Your first guess, that they may be the burnt remains of sacrificial victims, is quickly revised. The cinders are too dark and too heavy for that — more like volcanic ash. It is a vivid testimony of the unreasoning fanaticism of the Katak priesthood that they would collect and store such deposits in this quantity. Take one of the urns with you if you wish, then make your way back to the hall by turning to **288**.

53

You pass through a succession of high peaked chambers. To your right you see a cloistered gallery which runs the length of the wall and appears to link each chamber to the next. It is pointless to speculate on the reasoning behind Anku architecture, as it was guided more often by ritual and doctrine than by functional necessity. Nonetheless, as you walk on through the row of chambers you begin to think it might be worth going over to take a look at the gallery. If you wish to do so, turn to **236**. If you wish to continue west, turn to **217**.

54

The bodies of the cadavers lie around you in a debris of splintered weapons and riven armour. Your skin crawls at the sight of the pale, bloodless cuts your sword made in their grey flesh, but you force yourself to search them thoroughly. It is with some bitterness that you realize how needlessly

you prolonged the risky battle — you might as well have fled, for the cadavers carry nothing of value. Leaving through the opening in the south wall, you stride along a short passage and come to a halt before a door of black wood. With no other route available, you lift the latch and push the door open. Turn to **3**.

55

The passage brings you on to a low balcony overlooking a large circular chamber. The floor below is covered by a slowly dancing interplay of orange lights. As you watch, you see glowing patterns gradually unfold, blend and give way to new patterns in an unending display. You realize it must be caused by a patina of phosphor on the floor. Two curved staircases sweep down from either end of the balcony into the room. An archway leads off to the north about halfway down the right-hand staircase, and on the steps before this archway stand two worn statues.

If you wish to descend the staircase to your left, turn to **111.** If you would rather take the one to your right, turn to **16.**

56

You step through the doorway into a spacious hall with a high vaulted ceiling. Towering, fire blackened murals dominate the west and east walls. There is an open pit on the middle of the floor and a door at the far end.

You are striding briskly along the hall, being careful to give the pit a wide berth, when a noise wells up from deep in the earth that stops you dead. It begins as a faint howl of rushing wind, quickly building to a feral roar. A torrent of mingled fire and darkness erupts from the black maw of the pit. You step back aghast as you behold a gaunt figure of living shadow taking shape from the flames. It stands as high as the room, with its mane of smoke curling along the sloping roof and its eyes like embers against the soot-smeared stone. In one hand it holds a whip of sparks and in the other a scimitar-shaped jet of red flame.

It is the Malgash, the mightiest of all the demons of fire and evil. It steps forth in a rush of darkness and your swords clash — cold white light on hot red flame.

THE MALGASH   VIGOUR 18

Roll two dice:
score 2 to 7   You lose 4 VIGOUR
score 8 to 12   The Malgash loses 3 VIGOUR *and*
                      you lose 1 VIGOUR

Note that you lose a point of VIGOUR every time you hit the Malgash, because of the flames that cover its body. If you attempt to FLEE by running for the door in the north wall, roll as usual for its parting strike at you and then turn to **77**. If you fight and overcome it, turn to **256**.

57

Something is clearly amiss for the monkey to become so excited. You heft the rock he was sitting on and hurl it through the undergrowth in the direction you had originally intended to go. It lands with a dull plop and soon sinks from view. If you had not heeded the monkey's warning you would have blundered straight into a patch of deadly quicksand!

As you continue on your way, he runs alongside you and shows you the path of firm ground that takes you safely past the treacherous quicksand. With your new companion, whom you decide to call Minki, you head onwards through the jungle. After a little while you come to a trail of sorts, presumably beaten through the thick tropical undergrowth by the savage natives of the region. Although you hope to avoid any encounter with them, your hand never strays far from your sword hilt.

The trail soon brings you to a lichen-stained boulder sculpted to resemble a squatting figure with features that are both fierce and less than human. This weathered statue is clearly not the work of the natives. It has stood here for thousands of years and is a relic of the Ancient Empire of the Katak theocracy. Your knowledge of archaeology is limited, but if you read certain glyphs and baroque flourishes correctly then this statue marks the grave of an Anku nobleman. Possibly the treasure that would have been interred with him still remains undisturbed to this day.

Will you try to push the statue aside and open the grave (turn to **140**), or will you press on towards the lost temple (turn to **31**)?

58

The sceptre is heavy and ill-balanced. You wield it like a mace as the skullghasts glide closer to sear you with their enveloping flame.

Roll two dice:

score 2 to 3	You are grievously wounded; lose 6 VIGOUR
score 4 to 6	You are sorely wounded; lose 4 VIGOUR
score 7 to 9	You are wounded and lose 2 VIGOUR
score 10 to 12	One of the skullghasts shatters

You do not need to keep score of the skullghasts' VIGOUR as a single blow with the mace will smash one. If and when you have destroyed six of the creatures, turn to **206**.

59

The cadavers are almost upon you as you pull the drum from your backpack. The engravings on it depict warriors of the Anku Empire. In desperation, you begin to pound a beat on the drum with the flat of your hand. At once the cadavers stop advancing and begin a slow, macabre war-dance around you. As you move over to the south wall and along the passage, they follow you. You dare not stop the drumbeat that keeps them locked in their silent dance, so you head on with your uncanny retinue until you arrive at a large black door. There is no other way onwards. Still pounding the drum, you manage to lift the latch with your elbow and kick the door open. Turn to **218**.

60

Blue smoke curls up from the body at your feet. You realize the Phoenix's corpse is smouldering, about to catch light. If you have an urn full of cinders, you can use them to smother the corpse and prevent it from igniting. If you wish to do this, turn to **161**. If you do not have an urn of cinders, or do not wish to use it in this way, turn to **73**.

61

One of the natives had a small clay bottle tied on a thong around his wrist. It contains a pungent brown fluid which you recognize as snakebite antidote. You put it in your backpack and set off in search of the temple. Turn to **80**.

62

The gem is as smooth and as large as an egg, and gleams in your hand like a drop of blood. You do not have time to value it now, but it is of a very satisfying weight. You slip it into your backpack and head for the passage in the western wall. You are barely halfway across the room when brilliant light flares up in each of the niches. Minki cowers back against the wall.

You look upwards and can only stare in horror as the skulls – each now surrounded by a halo of lambent gold flame – float from their high eyries and swoop down towards you.

Are you wearing a jewelled pectoral? If so, turn to **192**. If you do not have this item, turn to **19**.

63

In the depths of its dark cowl, the Nightmare Guard hisses with cold glee as its garrotte snaps taut around your neck. Roll one die:

score 1	It breaks your neck; you die instantly
score 2 to 5	You struggle free but lose 2 VIGOUR
score 6	You get free without taking injury

If you are still alive, continue to fight.

Roll two dice:

score 2 to 5	Roll one die and refer to the above table
score 6 to 12	The Nightmare Guard loses 3 VIGOUR

As before, if you try to FLEE you should turn to **75**. If you kill the Nightmare Guard, turn to **166**.

64

The power of the ring renders you insubstantial for a few seconds – just long enough to step through the boulder into the corridor beyond. As you re-solidify, the ring crumbles in fragments from your finger. Cross it off your Character Sheet.

You hold up your sword and examine your surroundings. The corridor leads straight on ahead of you. In the dust you can see three sets of footprints – obviously those of Damontir and the two torchbearers, for where the Nightmare Guard

pass they leave no trace. You walk along the corridor which soon turns to head west. A little further along you come to a door in the wall to your left.

If you wish to open the door, turn to **167**. If you would rather carry straight on, turn to **269**.

65

There is a faint howl like wind across the moors as one of the Nightmare Guards turns to dust within its dark robe. The other only lunges forward again, and the corridor echoes as your blades clash.

Roll two dice:
score 2 to 5   You are hit and lose 3 VIGOUR
score 6 to 12   Your opponent loses 3 VIGOUR

If you win, you head north through the double doors. Turn to **108**.

66

You race frantically along the passage. There is no door or alcove where you might take cover, and the end of the passage is nowhere in sight. As you run, the creature takes careful aim at your back. You keep waiting for the bolt that will shrivel the flesh from your bones and scatter your blood in sizzling droplets. Searing energy lances through the air to strike your fleeing form. You are dead in less than a second.

67

You deposit the item you have chosen to leave in the statue's cupped hands and pick up the ebony drum. Remember to erase the item you have left from your Character Sheet. Examining the drum, , you see that it is encircled by angular carvings which portray warriors of the Anku Empire, their bodies twisted in a lusty, barbaric war-dance. You put the drum into your backpack and return to the vestibule to head west. Turn to **119**.

68

Your senses reel and you slump to the floor. Mercifully, you black out. You do not feel the elemental's red-hot gauntlets close upon you, or the bone-shattering impact with which it hurls you against the wall. Your life and your adventure end here.

69

You have not gone much further when the corridor you are in joins a second corridor running north and south. You decide to head straight on. Turn to **190**.

70

You break from cover and leap towards the startled sentries. They stare aghast at you, a resplendent and terrifying figure in your gleaming regalia of battle. Turn to **241** for the fight, but you may add 2 to your dice roll in the first Combat Round only, to represent your advantage of surprise.

71

The serpent shudders and spreads its plumage in a terrible hollow shriek. Sparkling crimson dust gushes forth from the many deep gashes your sword has cleaved in its stone body. The floor shakes as the serpent crashes down at your feet. Curious, you scoop up a handful of the dust these strange creatures bled. It is powdered ruby, perhaps imbued with magical properties. If you wish to fold some in a cloth and take it with you, you may do so. (Remember to note it on your Character Sheet if you do). Turn to **294**.

72

A passage off the far end of the gallery slopes gently upwards and eventually brings you to a small vestibule with triangular archways in the west and east walls. To the west you can see steps down, and decide to go that way.

Turn to **207**.

73

Your forehead beads with sweat in a sudden wave of heat. As you retreat from it, the corpse bursts into flame and is rapidly consumed. In moments, only glowing ashes remain. As you watch, the ashes begin to shift and stir, glowing ever more brightly until you finally have to avert your eyes from the blinding glare. As the light dims, you turn back and for a moment stand transfixed. The Phoenix has arisen, reborn from its ashes, all its wounds now healed. It towers over you, and its eyes are incandescent with proud fury. You realize that you must FLEE — either up the other staircase (turn to **4**) or east, along the tunnel under the balcony (turn to **220**).

74

A few hundred metres further on, the trail branches in two. If you wish to go right, turn to **95**. If you wish to go left, turn to **253**.

75

You have made a fatal mistake in turning your back on a master of the assassin's art. The silken garrotte slips down around your neck and, with a single deft twist, the Nightmare Guard extinguishes your life.

76

You place your sword on the floor beside you and seize the bars of the grille with both hands. Minki watches intrigued as you brace yourself to push at the grille with all your strength, pitting your flesh and bone against the corroded bronze and crumbling mortar. Suddenly the grille gives way, falling in on the dusty floor with a metallic clang. The noise echoes eerily along the hushed corridors. Passing along a short entrance tunnel, you find yourself in a narrow pillared chamber. There is another tunnel leading from the north wall directly opposite you. In the hot smoky light of two braziers (have they burned here since ancient times? were

the spells of the Anku priesthood so powerful?) you see a magnificent cloak of richly coloured feathers hanging at the far end of the room. Will you:

Take a closer look at the cloak?	Turn to **39**
Return to the passage and go on?	Turn to **213**
Cross over to the tunnel in the north wall?	Turn to **97**

77

You are almost at the door when the demon's terrible whip lashes out towards you. Roll one die. If you score 1 to 4, the whip curls around you — turn to **107**. If you score a 5 or 6, the whip cracks on empty air — turn to **235**.

78

You look through the contents of your backpack but cannot think of any item that might help. Once more you turn your gaze to the silver pyramid. Somewhere within or below it, you feel sure, lies the golden idol you have crossed half a world to find. In your imagination you see Damontir standing before it, his eyes lit with crazed greed as his fingers caress the sculpted metal. You groan in despair and the anguish of defeat, then slump to the jetty. With head bowed you watch the slow ripples drifting across the copper lake. You are so near to your goal and yet so far, and the taste of failure is bitter indeed.

79

The priest lords of the Anku Empire would hardly have left such a formidable monster in this room unless it was guarding something of great value or power. Sure enough, your search of the altar stone quickly uncovers a concealed recess in which lies an ornate golden chalice. You hold it up in the blue light cast by your sword and admire the intricate workmanship.

If you wish to pour some water into the chalice and drink

from it, turn to **109**. If not, you put it in your backpack for now and head west out of the room (turn to **87**).

80

Between the trees you discern the faintest signs of a straight path leading ahead. As you step forward you find you are treading upon ancient flagstones, green and springy with moss. This is not merely another of the crude native tracks. With Minki beside you, you walk steadfastly for about an hour, making good headway thanks to the centuries-old path you have found. It is now mid-afternoon. Your sun bronzed face is bathed in sweat. A thick curtain of lush fronds bars your way, and you push them aside to reveal a breathtaking sight.

In a vast clearing entirely free of vegetation, tier upon tier of grey basalt rise up before you. It is the magnificent pyramidal Temple of Katak, lost to civilization for twenty centuries! Hundreds of withered creepers choke the crumbling blocks and the broad flight of steps that ascends the pyramid's eastern face. In the shattered edifice at the summit you will find the entrance to the catacombs within.

You move quickly across the wide clearing to the pyramid's base. You are just about to start up the dusty stairway when you are brought up short by the sound of voices. To your amazement you see two men-at-arms strolling into view around one corner of the pyramid. They are about sixty metres away. Will you hail them (turn to **125**), or duck out of sight before they notice you (turn to **164**)?

81

You are lucky. Although you cannot see where you are going, you blunder straight into the pool. The cool water extinguishes the flames. Roll two dice — the score is the number of VIGOUR points you lose owing to burns. If you are still alive, you rise up laughing with relief and wade to the edge of the pool. You are disinclined to approach the statue again, so you leave and head west along the corridor. Turn to **119**.

82

You pull off your worn leather boots and eagerly buckle on the gold sandals. They are in fact the fabled Sandals of Talmiri, the Gladiator of the Gods, a hero in ancient times. They have the effect of increasing your *current* and *normal* AGILITY score to 10. Note down this change on your Character Sheet: your *normal* AGILITY is now 10. Elated by your chance discovery of such a potent magical prize, you walk back to the vestibule and head west along the corridor. Turn to **119**.

83

He hurls a black powder to the ground at his feet. You shield your eyes from a sudden glare of light and look up to find that he has transformed himself into a gruesome demon with rough horny skin and whirring wings of razor-sharp flint. You snatch your sword from your dumbfounded captor and raise it just in time to parry the first attack by this hideous adversary.

TRANSFORMED WITCHDOCTOR   VIGOUR 12

Roll two dice:
score 2 to 5   You are hit and lose 4 VIGOUR
score 6 to 12   The witchdoctor loses 3 VIGOUR

If you FLEE from the combat, turn to **189**. If you win, turn to **201**.

84

Your skin crawls at the fell revenant's touch, but you stare defiantly into its mould-clumped face and finally shrug off the virulent spell it is trying to cast upon you. Before it can prepare itself for a second attempt, you close your fingers on its ribcage and swing around to dash its brittle body against a hard stone pillar. It flies in fragments across the floor. You search for each bony shard and grind them all underfoot before picking up Minki and continuing west.

Turn to **217**.

85

Roll two dice (or roll one die twice and add the scores together). If the total is less than or equal to your current PSI, turn to **186**. If the total exceeds your PSI, turn to **247**.

86

Approaching the desecrated mummies, you see that the gold covering has been torn away from their faces. A few wisps of hair still cling to skin like cracked leather. Their eyes are narrow slits, but the black jaws of each gape in a sepulchral rictus. You stop before one of the mummies and gaze into its ancient face, experiencing a thrill of blended fear and fascination. Will you:

Examine the mummies more closely?	Turn to **104**
Continue along to the end of the hall?	Turn to **288**
Tear the gold covering from the face of one of the other mummies?	Turn to **232**

87

You walk along a featureless corridor for some time without finding a door or side tunnel. At last you come to the end of the corridor. Just as you are about to enter the room beyond, however, you notice a slight acrid smell in the air. When you glance back to see if Minki is still safely with you, you are surprised to see his fur bristling. As you approach the entrance of the room, the hairs on your own body start to prickle and stand on end.

If you wish to carry on into the room, turn to **92**. If you would prefer to turn back, turn to **250**.

88

Just as you are reaching for the skull, it suddenly ignites and floats up into the air — a grisly apparition wreathed in pale gold fire. If you are wearing a jewelled pectoral, turn to **234**. If you do not have this item, turn to **118**.

89

The corridor is soon joined by another from the south. Playing the blue light of your sword over the floor, you can make out three sets of footprints in the dust. They lead from the southern corridor and head west. You decide to follow them. Turn to **12**.

90

The powder is folded inside several large flat leaves. You tip it out on to your hand and examine it uncertainly. Having seen warlocks and magicians use magical dusts of transformation, you decide that that is what it must be. You concentrate on an image of yourself turning into an eagle and flying across the lake, then hurl the powder to the ground at your feet —

It is the last thing you ever know. Instead of rising in a magic cloud to transmute your body, the dust explodes on contact with the ground. The horrendous detonation rips you limb from limb and scatters you in a gory smear across the walls and the lake's surface. You should never have tried experimenting with the contents of a witchdoctor's medicine pouch!

91

You soon arrive at the end of the tunnel. There is nothing but a blank stone wall in front of you. You are about to retrace your steps to explore a different route when, acting on a hunch, you tap the wall with your sword-hilt and discover that it is hollow. It is, in fact, a secret door, and you soon discover that by applying pressure at one edge you can

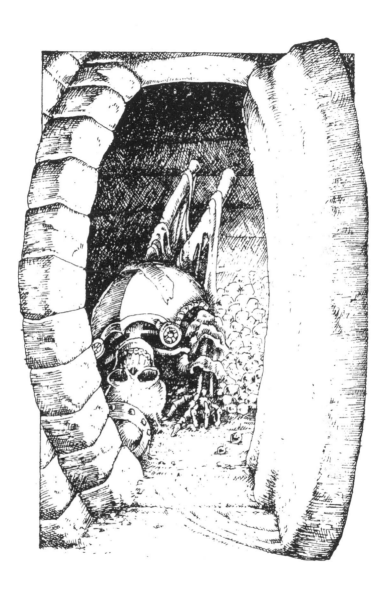

cause it to pivot around a central hinge. Beyond, you see a small room in which a dusty skeleton sprawls beside a pile of sparkling gems. If you wish to enter this room, turn to **153**. If you would rather return to the Phoenix's lair and make your way up to the other staircase, turn to **16**.

92

As you cross the threshold into the room, there comes a harsh sound like a ship's mast snapping and a bolt of magical lightning crackles from the walls to engulf you. For a moment your muscles lock rigid and you are held in a paroxysm of pain. As the coruscating light around you fades, you are released from your paralysis to fall forward into the room. Lose 5 VIGOUR.

If you are still alive, you lie in the dust for a few moments while the memory of your torture fades. Your mouth is dry and you feel quite weak. Minki is beside you, pawing at your arm. In spite of the pain, you are glad that he was behind you. If the bolt had discharged through his small frame then it would surely have killed him. You manage to stand up on quivering legs (reduce your AGILITY by 1 point) and look around you. You are in a wide, shadowy hall which may once have served as a convocation chamber for the worshippers of Katak. The floor is shrouded under centuries of dust. As you move further into the room, the light of your sword falls upon two bronze-bound doors to the west. There seems to be no other way on from the hall, so you cross to these doors. Will you open the one to your left (turn to **150**) or the one to your right (turn to **134**)?

93

A number of passages and side chambers lead off the hall, but you decide it would be fruitless to explore all of these. Continuing on, you leave through the high archway at the western end of the hall and walk along the corridor beyond until it turns to head south. Directly ahead of you is an opening in the wall, and through it you can see steps leading down. You can go down the steps (turn to **263**) or stay in the corridor and head south (turn to **194**).

94

Spurred by your fear, you execute a leap of extraordinary agility and land on a nearby outcropping. White flame streams from the dragon's snout to lick around the rock you have just vacated. You see it throw up a cloud of sizzling water droplets from the lake surface.

The dragon may breathe again at any moment, and you have little time to deliberate on your next move. With your way to the arch barred, will you take on the fearsome beast with your sword (turn to **182**) or will you use an item you have found (turn to **148**)?

95

As you stride on through the jungle, you do not see the snare that is set across your path. Suddenly it goes taut around your ankle as the tree to which it is attached whips upright. You are jerked clear of the ground and dangle helplessly. There is a dull twang as the second part of this native trap is sprung — a heavy barbed spear hurtles through the air towards you.

To avoid it you must roll equal to or less than your current AGILITY score on two dice. If you succeed, turn to **137**. If the combined roll of the two dice exceeds your AGILITY, turn to **196**.

96

You enter a large room from which a single passage leads west. As you make your way across to this, you notice a massive granite block against the opposite wall. It may once have been an altar to Katak, where the ferocious god's priests would have butchered heretics and war captives. You are just about to head over to the altar to search it for hidden treasure when a bizarre creature lopes out of the shadows to confront you. It is bipedal, with dark spiky skin and vestigial forelimbs, but its most unusual feature is its 'head', for this is actually no more than a huge glowing eye on the end of a long stalk. As you hesitate, transfixed by its odd appearance, the creature discharges a searing beam of ruby light from its eye. You start to move, but you are too slow. The energy blast rips sinew and fusing your bones to a tarry mess. You are dead before you have time to scream.

97

It is a short tunnel just like the one in the opposite wall of the chamber, ending in another bronze grille. Peering through the bars you see a passage stretching into the darkness to your left and right. You could get through into the passage by forcing the grille. As before, it will cost you 1 point of VIGOUR. If you wish to force the grille open, subtract 1 from your *current* VIGOUR score and turn to **266**. If you decide against that, you may now inspect the cloak of feathers (turn to **39**) or return to the other passage and head on (turn to **213**).

98

With each moment the undead warriors become stronger and faster, while your own fatigue begins to tell. You fight on with instinctive skill as you weigh up the arguments favouring a strategic withdrawal.

Roll two dice:

score 2 to 3	You lose 6 VIGOUR
score 4 to 6	You lose 3 VIGOUR
score 7 to 12	One of the cadavers loses 3 VIGOUR

If you decide to FLEE, turn to **15** (remember that both the cadavers will get a last strike at you). If you choose to fight on and manage to overcome another, turn to **238**.

99

It is getting difficult to breathe. Your muscles feel like water and you pitch forward into the heaped bones. You have not even enough strength to cry out. Your own bones will soon join those on which you lie. Even in death, the scorpion has claimed you as its final victim.

100

The spiral staircase takes you down a long way. You realize as you reach the bottom at last that you are now deep underground, far below the pyramid itself. You think back upon the last few hours — you have escaped bizarre perils, conquered monsters more grotesque than any you have faced before. And, in Minki, you have won and lost a valued companion. Damontir's wrongs must not continue unpunished. Strangely, there is no dust here to show you his footprints — you have no evidence that he survived to get this far, but somehow you know he is ahead of you. His spells and devious cunning will have brought him safely through the temple, but they will not save him from you.

Directly ahead, in the north wall of the chamber in which you stand, a marble portico encloses an archway from which light streams. You cross the floor and pass through into the room beyond.

Turn to **130**.

101

The potion feels cold as it trickles down your throat. Within moments, a surge of energy courses through your whole body. If you are wounded, the potion restores 20 points of VIGOUR. However, this will *not* increase your VIGOUR above its *normal* score — any excess points are simply wasted. You throw the empty bottle aside. Return to the last entry you were reading.

There is a sound from inside the ruined structure atop the pyramid. Wasting no time, you vault over a fallen column and land with catlike grace within the broken ruins. A glance takes in the details — a bored sentry leaning against the wall, a spear in the crook of his arm, his hands folded across his pot belly — his companion, slumped in the shade under the portico, snoring beneath a wide-brimmed hat while flies tread in the dampness of his pasty face. You do not even trouble to unsheathe your sword. Two strides bring you face to face with the first man. He stares at you in slack-jawed astonishment and then doubles up as your fist slams into his sternum. A second blow completes the job. His limp body falls to the masonry-strewn floor like a broken doll.

You catch his spear and turn to face the other man. Rhythmic snores still emanate from under the brim of his hat. You heft the spear and advance on him. You would like to spit him like a pig where he lies, but that is not the way of the Knights of Palados. You are about to yell at him to wake up when Minki darts forward and prods him in the eye. Spluttering, the man is roused from his slumber. As soon as he sees you he draws his sword and jumps up to fight.

SENTRY   VIGOUR 9

Roll two dice:
score 2 to 3   You are hit and lose 3 VIGOUR
score 4 to 12   The sentry loses 3 VIGOUR

If you win, turn to **216**.

You set your backpack down on the floor and leave Minki squatting on top of it as you jump across on to the plinth. To your relief, it does not shift or drop away under your weight. Nor does there seem to be any kind of trap on the casket, as far as you can tell. However, the moment you open the rusted clasp and lift the lid, a thick cloud of jet-black vapour billows out around you. If you wish to jump back out of the vapour, turn to **114**. If you would prefer to hold your breath and find out what is inside the casket, turn to **229**.

104

Despite some misgivings, you peel more of the gold leaf from the nearest mummy in order to examine it more carefully. You lay bare a shrivelled body graced with many fine jewels and artefacts. If Damontir exposed the faces of several mummies, you wonder, why did he not also loot their bodies of this treasure? You have your answer, perhaps, as a sense of fearful doom suddenly assails you. The priest-kings wove a sorcerous defence about themselves, and their curse is reaching down to you through the centuries. Fortunately the curse has been weakened by the passage of time, and you need only roll your current PSI or less on *one* die to resist it. If you succeed, turn to **33**. If you fail, turn to **38**.

105

You take a brand from the open fire where the village women are cooking and use it to torch the huts. The dry reeds burn furiously in the scorching afternoon heat. You wrest the witchdoctor's bone wand from him so that he cannot send any magic after you, and then release him. As he stamps and shrieks, the natives abandon any attempt to tend the blaze and take up their spears and blowpipes. It seems they are determined to have their revenge on you, even if that means letting the village burn down. A poisoned dart whistles past your ear! Turn to **189**.

106

The dust around you lies smooth and undisturbed, broken only by your own footprints and Minki's pawmarks. The spectral warriors have gone as though they never existed, but the wounds they dealt you prove they were no mere phantasms of your mind. Chilled by the memory of the ghostly battle, you continue west.

Turn to **293**.

107

The whip scorches the leather of your armour and burns into your flesh like white-hot drops of lead. You scream in pain as you are dragged back towards the fire demon. Lose 5 VIGOUR and, if you are still alive, turn to **282**.

108

Shortly you arrive at a narrow flight of steps which you follow downwards. Turn to **207**.

109

If you are wounded, turn to **225**. If your VIGOUR score is currently undepleted, on the other hand, then turn to **177**.

110

Your last blow smashes the loathsome revenant asunder. You crush the bony fragments underfoot. At last, when all that remains is a debris of powder and fine shards, your battle-rage subsides.

Turn to **93**.

111

You reach the bottom of the staircase and see that a tunnel leads east in the wall below the balcony. As you step further into the room, a terrifying shrill cry shatters the silence and a majestic Phoenix spreads its wings before you. It seems to have appeared out of nowhere — from above, its brick red plumage blended with the flickering phosphorescence. The feathers on the underside of its wings and across its breast are bright gold and its curved beak shines like metal. You recover from your astonishment barely in time to dodge its first attack and draw your sword.

PHOENIX   VIGOUR 12

Roll two dice:
score 2 to 6   You are hit; lose 3 VIGOUR
score 7 to 12   The Phoenix loses 3 VIGOUR

If you FLEE up the other staircase, turn to **4**. If you win, turn to **21**.

112

You hit the lake on your back and, stunned by the impact, sink like a stone in the boiling waters. Your flesh is scalded raw within seconds, but you seem almost detached from the convulsing pain. Images of a slow billowing inferno engulf you, and in the midst of them looms the cruel visage of Damontir the Mad. Thus, at the end, your thoughts are of the man for whom you have borne such hatred through the years. You will never exact retribution now, never avenge poor Minki's death. Damontir's triumphant laughter torments your final moments as you boil to death in the depths of the lake.

113

The remaining sentry watches in terror as you cut down his comrade. Throwing down his sword, he sprints for the edge of the clearing. Minki chases him a little of the way, screeching abusively and hurling nutshells, then gives up and scampers back to your side. You watch as the fleeing sentry wades into the jungle and is lost to view. He clearly prefers to take his chances with the natives and wild beasts than face you in single combat. Wise choice. You slip your blade back into its scabbard and bend to examine the other man's corpse. You find 8 gold coins and a hipflask of gin. Take what you will and then head up the pyramid steps by turning to **200**.

114

You jump back instinctively as the vapour engulfs you. Your only thought is to keep it from getting in your lungs, and you forget all about the pit until you find yourself toppling backwards off the plinth. You try to twist in mid-air, but dash your head against the side of the pit and plunge heavily to the bottom. When you come to, you are in darkness. Your glowing sword still lies on the plinth above. In its faint blue light you see Minki peering down anxiously. Your first attempt at moving sends a wave of sickening pain up your leg. You have twisted it badly and must reduce your *current* AGILITY score by 2 points.

This comes at a particularly inopportune time as you will need to be agile if you are to scale the rough, chiselled walls of the pit. You get painfully to your feet and begin the long climb up.

Roll two dice. If the total is less than or equal to your current AGILITY score, turn to **197**. If the total of the two dice exceeds your AGILITY, turn to **138**.

115

You crash forward and break your neck on the hard stone steps. Your death is instantaneous, and a better fate by far then that you would have received at the hands of the accursed smoke wraiths.

116

A short stretch of corridor opens into a tall conical room faced with grey-white marble. A multitude of deep recesses indent the walls, and in each stands a stoppered bronze urn stained with an azure bloom of corrosion. There is no other way on from this room, so you may either return to the Hall of the priest-kings and select another route (turn to **288**) or try opening one of the urns (turn to **52**).

117

As you begin the opening feints and thrusts in this uneven battle, you catch sight of someone moving between the trees. It is the girl you freed. The natives see her also, and for some reason this makes them blanch. The girl pads forward through the leaves, gathering speed. She drops to a crouch, then to all fours. As she races towards you, her glistening olive skin seems to take up the pattern of the dappled sunlight that falls upon it. There is a deep growl that could not come from a human throat. Suddenly a lithe tawny jaguar crashes through the undergrowth on to the path, sending the natives fleeing in abject terror. The jaguar looks at you and Minki and then slowly prowls off into the jungle. The girl you freed was a Werecat, a lycanthrope whom the natives had bound with silver and caged for their own safety. She has repaid your kindness in freeing her by possibly saving your life.

You are about to proceed when you notice a small clay bottle lying on the trampled grass. One of the natives dropped it when he ran. It contains a pungent brown fluid which you identify as snakebite antidote. You put it in your backpack (write it on your Character Sheet) and set off in search of the temple. Turn to **80**.

118

You barely have time to bring your sword up to parry the skullghast as it swoops towards you. Yellow flames form a crackling halo around it, but its snapping jaws are as black as an open tomb.

SKULLGHAST VIGOUR 6

Roll two dice:
score 2 to 5   You are burned; lose 2 VIGOUR
score 6 to 12   The skullghast loses 3 VIGOUR

If you win, turn to **155**. If you FLEE from this room and try the other door instead, throw the dice as usual and then turn to **150**.

119

You soon find yourself in an echoing pillared hall. Do you have a jewelled pectoral? If so, turn to **251**. If you do not have this item, turn to **93**.

120

The dark, cowled figures of perhaps a dozen Nightmare Guards cluster forward from the archway. In their midst stands the warlock Damontir. He is little changed by the gulf of years since your last meeting. The sallow face and artful smile are the same, the long white hair swept back from the widow's peak, the pentagram tattoo around his left eye. The glint of insane evil in his gaze.

Damontir slowly draws off one of his velvet gauntlets to reveal a sparkling jewel — the Ring of Red Ruin. 'I would prefer to savour this moment,' he says, 'but I am in haste to acquire the idol. Your death will be but a brief and squalid interlude.'

You watch grimly as he levels the magical ring at you. There is a pause of several heartbeats. Surely he does not expect you to cringe before him! You tense up, ready to drop low and rush them, but when the blast comes it is not meant for you. The coruscating flame lances from Damontir's ring to strike poor Minki from your shoulder! The mad warlock cackles inhumanly as the monkey's charred body drops from the walkway into the white clouds far below.

Your shocked paralysis at this sudden and needless slaughter lasts only a second, and then you are charging along the walkway, swinging your flashing sword and roaring in blood-rage. Damontir blanches and steps back, no longer laughing. You halt close to the ledge as the Nightmare Guard move in to protect their master. You adopt a defensive stance and wait for them to come to you. The narrow walkway is to your advantage: they can only fight you one at a time.

Damontir, however, has other plans. Recovering his composure, he orders the Nightmare Guard back and calls out to you, saying, 'There is another member of my retinue. I believe you knew him once as Sulsa Doom.'

Two scared-looking slaves step forward into the arch behind Damontir. The guttering light of the torches they carry illuminates a figure waiting there. He stands more than two metres tall, with a huge falchion in each grey hand. His armour shows patches of rust and a mouldering cloak swathes him like a shroud. He advances stiffly on to the walkway.

'It cannot be Doom!' you say, knowing that it is. 'A score of knights saw him topple from the Tower of Victory when his attack on the king was thwarted!'

'My servants retrieved the body and I used necromancy to reanimate it. Sulsa Doom is no more than a mindless zombie now, but his skills as a warrior are undiminished — as you will discover. Doom, slay this fool then guard the way until I Return.' Damontir and his black agents turn to leave, but he lingers just a moment in the archway to murmur equably, 'Farewell, Dragon Knight. You must excuse me for saying it, but I think your doom is at last upon you.'

His laughter echoes back as he walks off into the darkness. Turn to **160**.

121

You raise the small clay vial to your lips and pause. The green liquid could be anything — a magical potion, as you hope, or a deadly poison which could kill you in an instant. But, in spite of the risk, you hesitate for no more than a second. You must stop Damontir whatever the cost to yourself, and if the witchdoctor's sorcery cannot get you across the lake then nothing will.

You gulp the liquid down, then scream as a terrible pain twists your limbs. Sweat pours from you. You stare at your quaking hands through a red glare of agony. You hear yourself screaming again and again, but your mind feels strangely clear and almost distant from the pain as you watch your hands forming into claws! Abruptly, your torment ceases. You look around at a scene which seems subtly altered — but it is you who have changed. To your astonishment, you find that you are now a green and gold quetzal bird! You spread your wings and launch yourself out off the jetty. The experience of flight is a thrill you can barely believe, and you skim across the lake to the silver pyramid. The moment you land on the bottom step, the transformation reverses itself — this time painlessly — and moments later you are yourself again. Turn to **270**.

122

You walk along a narrow passage with only the wan, magical light from your sword to show you the way. Stalking figures in bas-relief form a martial frieze along the walls. After a short time you come to a bronze grille set across an opening in the wall to your right. Minki clambers upon the metal bars, chattering excitedly. Ahead of you the passage recedes into the darkness. If you wish to go on, turn to **213**. If you wish to try and break the grille down, turn to **157**.

123

Your strength deserts you before you are even halfway. Senses reeling, you slump to the floor. As your vision blurs and fades, the last thing you see is the row of carved faces along the wall. They stare down, sightless and uncaring, at your tortured death throes. You have failed in your quest.

124

You hurl the spear at the approaching dragon with all your strength. The spear flashes through the air and sinks deep into the dragon's left eye. The great reptile's roar of pain reverberates up the shaft as it thrashes about and tries to grip the spear with its taloned claws. When it rips the spear out at last, you see a wash of coppery blood on its red scales. It roars again as it fixes its good eye upon you. You hastily raise your sword to battle the wounded monster as it surges through the churning waters towards you.

RED DRAGON   VIGOUR 18

Roll two dice:
score 2 to 5	You are wounded; lose 4 VIGOUR
score 6 to 12	The dragon loses 3 VIGOUR

There is no opportunity to FLEE past it. If you win, turn to **159**.

125

The two men respond to your shout of greeting by unlimbering their crossbows. You realize why as you draw nearer and focus on the insignia they wear — they are retainers of the crazed warlock Damontir. Somehow your hated foe has beaten you to the temple. His nefarious sorcery would account for the strange amnesia of the old librarian in Achtan.

You have no time to ponder the matter further — the two men are cranking up their bows. Grasping your sword you pound across the red, sun-baked earth towards them, bellowing out your ferocious war cry as you run. With trembling hands they level their crossbows, aware that you will be upon them in seconds. Roll one die for their shots:

score 1	Turn to **228**
score 2 or 3	Both quarrels hit; you lose 6 VIGOUR
score 4 or 5	Only one hits you; lose 3 VIGOUR
score 6	Both shots go wide

If you are still alive, you close with them as they discard the crossbows and draw their swords. Turn to **241**.

You watch the skullghasts carefully, quickly learning to spot the slight intensification of aura that indicates when one of them is about to swoop closer and burn you with its fire. You will need all your skill to defeat them.

Each skullghast has a VIGOUR score of 6.

Roll two dice:

score 2	You are grievously wounded; lose 6 VIGOUR
score 3 to 4	You are sorely wounded; lose 4 VIGOUR
score 5 to 7	You are wounded and lose 2 VIGOUR
score 8 to 12	One of the skullghasts loses 3 VIGOUR

If and when you have destroyed six of the creatures, turn to **206**.

Casting the ruby dust in their lifeless faces does nothing to halt the cadavers' relentless advance. They are almost upon you, and you can do nothing now but fight them. Turn to **41**.

It takes you barely a second to reach the slab, though that interval seems an eternity as you watch the gap inexorably closing. There is now just half a metre between the floor and the descending slab. You dive, rolling on the ancient flagstones.

Throw two dice. If the total exceeds your current AGILITY, turn to **17**. If the total is equal to or less than your AGILITY, turn to **212**.

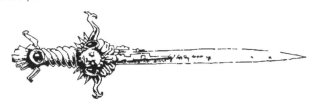

You have gone only a short distance further when you are brought up short by two native warriors who step out to block your path. Their faces are hideously tattooed and yellow war-paint forms a flame-design on their smooth chests. You step back slowly and start to turn, only to find that another native has crept up behind you. They level their spears and circle around you, baring their filed teeth in bloodthirsty smiles. They are savage cannibals who will fight you to the death.

FIRST NATIVE   VIGOUR 9
SECOND NATIVE VIGOUR 9
THIRD NATIVE   VIGOUR 6

Roll two dice:
score 2 to 3   You are hit and lose 9 VIGOUR
score 4 to 5   You are hit and lose 6 VIGOUR
score 6 to 7   You are hit and lose 3 VIGOUR
score 8 to 12   One of the natives (you choose which) loses 3 VIGOUR

If you kill one, turn to **258** to continue the fight.

You find yourself in a cavernous hallway of ochre stone illuminated by the flickering luteous glow of thousands of candles that stand in ornate brazen racks. The walls to either side slant up to a vast, gilded ceiling supported by a line of monumental pillars along the centre of the hall. Niches in the walls, bordered by carved glyphs of painstaking complexity, contain mummified bodies wrapped in gold leaf. You must be in the burial chamber of the priest-kings of the Anku Empire.

As you pass along the echoing hall towards the exits at the northern end, you notice that the gold leaf has been ripped away from several of the mummies. If you wish to go over and investigate, turn to **86**. If you would rather walk on down the hall, turn to **288**.

131

You should have left the dagger where it lay — Damontir would hardly have dropped it by accident. As you hold it, the image of bright metal and black leather hilt fade away. It is no longer a dagger you see before you, but a crawling jungle spider, transformed for a while by Damontir's magic and left here as a trap for you. You cry out and hurl the spider away — too late to avoid its bite. Your wrist burns with pain as you hurriedly cut at the wound with your knife. Lose 7 points of VIGOUR. If you are still alive, you crush the revolting creature under the heel of your boot. Still weak from the effects of its poison, you stumble on along the corridor. Turn to **190**.

132

You reach the bottom of the stairs and hurl yourself aside. The flagstone at the foot of the staircase shatters as the boulder hits it, throwing up a spray of rock shards. You feel the floor quake under you as the boulder rumbles across the room and smashes into the wall. Turn to **211**.

133

You find yourself in a small chamber from which the only passage leads north. You make for this, only to whirl in alarm as the doors slam shut behind you. Two of Damontir's Nightmare Guard lurked unnoticed in the shadows behind the doors, and one of them now leaps forward and sinks its slender knife into your arm before you can defend yourself. Lose 3 VIGOUR and, if you are still alive, turn to **249**.

134

The door opens into a small room with no other exits. There is a black marble pedestal on which rests a grinning skull. If you wish to step into the room to examine the skull, turn to **88**. If you wish to close this door and try the other one, turn to **150**.

135

You go straight to the cavity in the wall where the elemental was imprisoned. A hot sulphurous stench wafts from it. Inside you can see a black ceramic ring. When you hook this out on the point of your sword and examine it, you find it bears a red glyph in the shape of the sun's disc. The ring is still very hot after its exposure to the elemental's flame and, since you cannot afford to waste time waiting for it to cool, you will have to quench it with water from your hipflask if you wish to take it with you. If you decide to do that, record on your Character Sheet that you have used up all your water and turn to **172**. If you do not want the ring, you may leave it here and return to the main corridor to head south (turn to **194**).

136

A short, downward-sloping tunnel opens on a spectacle that takes your breath away. You are standing on a jutting ledge on one side of a shaft nearly fifty metres across! It must go right down into the heart of the pyramid — perhaps deeper than that. You cannot see the bottom for billowing clouds of steam rise up the shaft. A stone walkway, improbably narrow and impossibly unsupported, spans the width of the shaft to a ledge on the eastern wall. Through the seething vapour you can see the black mouth of an archway leading from the other ledge. The walls of the shaft are filmed with rippling water, which is perhaps flowing in along ducts in the pyramid from the tropical storm above. It streams down into the depths of the shaft. Far below, you imagine a spring or underground lake. After allowing yourself a moment or two to take in this staggering vista, you concede that the only way onwards lies across the narrow walkway. Minki clings nervously to your shoulder as you step out on to it.

You are slightly more than two-thirds of the way across when, from the archway ahead, a cry rings out above the insistent murmur of trickling water: 'Ah, Dragon Knight! The flower of Paladosian chivalry! And I, the blight that will wither the bloom.'

The voice is Damontir's.

Turn to **120**.

137

You manage to twist yourself out of the way of the spear at the last moment. It whistles past you and embeds itself in the bole of a nearby tree. You watch the bushes slowly swaying under your head and begin to wonder how you are going to free yourself. An insistent chattering attracts your attention. Craning your neck, you see that Minki has climbed the tree. He is carrying your knife, which you dropped when you set off the snare. He slides down the rope and you gratefully take the knife from him. It takes you only a few seconds to twist yourself into an upright position, cut through the rope around your ankle, and jump down to the ground. You put Minki on your shoulder and continue along the track.

Turn to **267**.

138

You lose your grip on the cracked rock walls and plummet back into the pit with a startled cry. Lose 4 VIGOUR points.

If you are still alive, you can only try again to climb up out of the pit. As before, you must try to roll equal to or less than your current AGILITY on two dice. If you succeed, turn to **197**. If you fail, you will fall again (losing another 4 VIGOUR points) and must continue to try until you either manage the climb or die trying.

139

Lose 3 more points of PSI. If your *current* PSI had dropped to 0 or less now, turn to **247**. Otherwise, you stagger on and suddenly emerge from the smoke into clean air. You look back to see the smoke cloud writhing on the steps behind you like a living thing. As your panic dies, the full harrowing horror of your experience settles on you. You find yourself trembling uncontrollably as you continue downwards. Turn to **100.**

140

You put your shoulder to the statue and heave. It seems rooted to the spot. At last your titanic effort is rewarded as the statue topples, crashing down into a thicket. Lose 1 VIGOUR for your exertion in the sweltering heat. You have uncovered the stone lid of a sarcophagus in the dank earth beneath the fallen statue. Maggots and tiny black beetles squirm and scuttle for cover. Minki snatches up a beetle and savours it while you stoop to examine the sarcophagus. You seize the carved handholds and open the lid.

At that instant, a momentary breeze stirs the trees and makes you shiver. Minki runs back from the grave, chattering in fright. But there is nothing to fear, only the mouldering bones of a long-dead Anku noble. The skeleton could be formed of polished jade, coated as it is with a lime green enamel which has preserved it through the centuries. It holds a gilded sceptre in one hand and wears a pectoral from which sparkling jewels hang like crystallized droplets. You can take either or both of these items; remember to note them on your Character Sheet if you do. Turning away from the rifled grave, you and Minki proceed deeper into the entangling jungle.

Turn to **31.**

141

From the footprints in the dust in the passage you know that your enemy has found a way across the lake of copper. So must you. Perhaps you have a witchdoctor's medicine pouch? If so, turn to **2**. If not, turn to **78**.

142

You walk along the narrow passage, your every step stirring up dust which filters the light of your sword eerily. Bas-relief figures stand out from the walls — warriors marching to a flowery death. After some distance you pass an opening in the wall to your left. It is blocked by a heavy bronze grille and, since you can see nothing but a bare, dusty tunnel beyond it, you decide to continue heading west. Eventually you enter a large room where savage carvings merge with the walls and pillars.

Turn to **257**.

143

You reach out your hand...

Turn to **259**.

144

Even before you hand has touched the drum, twin beams of dazzling light stab from the statue's opal eyes. The beams ignite your armour within seconds. Shrouded in leaping flames, you back away. You stumble blindly across the room, shrieking wildly as the fire blisters your skin. Your only hope lies in finding the pool. Roll one die. If you score 1 to 3, turn to **289**. If you score 4 to 6, turn to **81**.

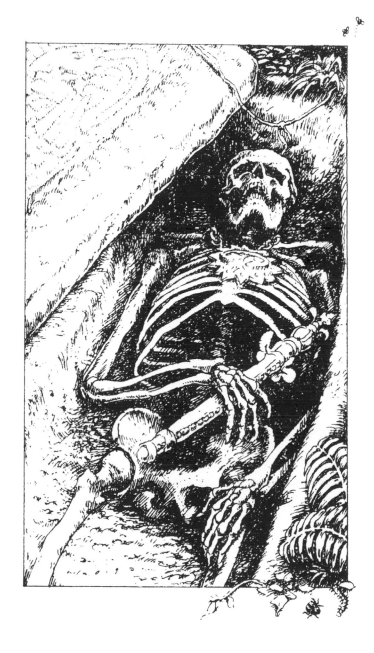

145

None of the other wonders of the Temple of Katak can have prepared you for this sight. You step from the gloom of the passage on to a stone jetty beside a fabulous lake of liquid copper. Ahead of you across the shimmering surface rises a replica of the pyramid itself, some eight metres high and wrought entirely of silver. Its stepped facade sparkles in the brilliant glare of light globules that float mysteriously about in the air. Though staggered to behold such unimaginable riches, you remember that you have come seeking something of still greater value — the lost idol of Katak — and even now your enemy may be approaching it.

You stare out over the molten lake. How are you to cross it? If you have a black pearl, turn to **219**. If you did not come across such an item on your quest, turn to **141**.

146

There is another bronze grille at the end of this tunnel. As before, forcing the grille will cost you 1 point of VIGOUR. If you wish to force the grille open and head west along the passage on the other side of it, turn to **266** (remembering to deduct the point of VIGOUR). Otherwise, you may return to the passage you were in before and head on (turn to **213**).

147

You pause by a face whose jaw is set in a look of truculent arrogance. Alert for traps or poison spikes, you reach into its mouth and probe the space within. Your fingers quickly find a small hole, far too narrow for you to get your hand into. You shrug and step back from the wall. The face glowers sightlessly back at you. Intending to continue along the tunnel, you turn. Then you notice the stifling heat. Your breath comes in short shallow gasps, but you cannot seem to get any air. You start to run back the way you came, but your legs give way and you crash to the floor. The sword slips from your enfeebled grasp and, with your strength gone, you cannot rise. The only sound is the tortured sobbing of your breath in the oxygen-starved air. Soon that too is silenced. Your adventure ends here.

148

Which of your items will you try:

A spear?	Turn to **124**
A gilded sceptre?	Turn to **252**
Powdered ruby?	Turn to **264**

If you have none of these, you must fight: turn to **182**.

149

One of the crossbow quarrels punctures your lung. You are abruptly drained of strength and fall helplessly on the oven-hot stone steps. Disjointed shouts and fragments of memories jostle at the edge of consciousness. You are aware of Minki tugging at your cloak with his tiny paws as you sprawl amid the weathered chunks of masonry, coughing your lifeblood on to the ancient ruins. Grotesque carvings leer at you from either side of the stairway. You try to drag yourself up the remaining steps, but the world is spinning around you and you no longer have any idea whether you are going up or down. It seems that a cloud covers the sun as the shadow of oblivion settles on you. Damontir's sentries will see to it that you never awaken.

150

A gust of wind arises as if from nowhere as you swing the door open. The thick dust ripples like the surface of a lake and then rises up to form three translucent columns around you. Images take shape within the swirling motes. At first you think it is a trick of the light, but then you see glimmering eyes like candle flames and swords like shafts of moonlight. Three spectral warriors surround you, ghosts from ages past. You must pray that the magic in your shining sword is enough to lay these murderous phantoms.

First SPECTRAL WARRIOR	VIGOUR 9
Second SPECTRAL WARRIOR	VIGOUR 9
Third SPECTRAL WARRIOR	VIGOUR 9

Roll two dice:

score 2 to 3	You are hit three times; lose 9 VIGOUR *and* 1 PSI
score 4 to 5	You are hit twice; lose 6 VIGOUR
score 6 to 7	You are hit once; lose 3 VIGOUR
score 8 to 12	One of the spectral warriors (you choose which) loses 3 VIGOUR

They surround you and so you cannot FLEE. If you destroy one of them, note the VIGOUR scores of the other two and then turn to **181**.

151

The revenant manages to seize you by the arm. You can feel its skeletal fingers biting deep into your flesh, followed by a tingling sensation through your whole body. Roll two dice. If the score is less than or equal to your current PSI score, turn to **84**. If the score exceeds your PSI, turn to **243**.

152

A winding passage takes you steadily west and eventually emerges into a small vestibule. From here, a narrow passage heads north and steps lead down from the west wall. You decide to go down the steps. Turn to **207**.

153

As you step through, the secret door swings shut behind you with a dull and ominous crunch. You immediately attempt to open it again, but it will not budge for all your pummelling and pounding. At last, exhausted by your futile efforts, you sit down on the floor. You are trapped. Falling into a spirit of wry fatalism, you allow yourself a bitter smile as you lift a handful of gems and watch them trickle through your fingers. Like the skeleton beside you, you have stumbled upon the lavish riches of the priest-kings' treasure vault but will never escape to enjoy your wealth. Already it is getting difficult to breathe. This sealed chamber will be your tomb.

154

You stand in an antechamber from which two passages lead west. Incomprehensible votive carvings cover every inch of the walls. As you step off the dais it rises back up to the roof, sealing out the daylight and the hiss of falling rain. You hold out your enchanted sword before you. A blue radiance shimmers from its blade, illuminating your surroundings and throwing the carvings on the near wall into sharp relief. Which way will you go from here:

Along the left-hand passage?	Turn to **272**
Along the right-hand passage?	Turn to **142**

155

The second blow of your enchanted sword shivers the undead monster into a hundred fragments. You search the room thoroughly but can find nothing of interest, so you return to the hall and try the other door.

Turn to **150**.

156

You find yourself in a vaulted vestibule with brass double doors directly ahead of you and, to your left, a corridor leading west. If you wish to try the doors, turn to **170**. If you would rather head along the corridor, turn to **119**.

157

The effort will cost you 1 point of VIGOUR. If you wish to do it, deduct this from your *current* VIGOUR score and turn to **76**. If you have now changed your mind and wish to continue along the passage, turn to **213**.

You soon discover that the plug is wedged tightly into the wall, requiring several jarring blows with your sword-pommel to loosen it. No sooner have you unstoppered the hole in the wall than a jet of red flame leaps out of it towards your face. You drop the heavy plug and dodge back with a cry of alarm, flinching at the fierce heat as the fire streams past you like molten ruby. Watching the flame spiral across the room, you feel sure there is an image within it — a flickering orange lizard running on thin air. Suddenly the visor of the bronze armour snaps up and the fiery salamander scuttles into it. The visor shuts again with a harsh clang. The armour's eye-slit burns with the glow of hellfire now. From it comes the furnace-roar of air being drawn through the visor to feed the inferno within. As you bring your sword-blade up, the armour steps from the alcove and moves ponderously towards you.

FIRE ELEMENTAL   VIGOUR 12

Roll two dice:
score 2 to 6   You are hit; lose 3 VIGOUR
score 7 to 12   The fire elemental loses 3 VIGOUR

If you FLEE into the tunnel, turn to **292**. If you decide to stand and fight, turn to **29** after three Combat Rounds.

You watch the steaming waters close over the Dragon's carcass. Its blood is a copperish scum on the surface of the lake. When it has sunk from sight in the turbid depths and the lake is still once more, you continue along the line of rocks to the arch in the north wall. Turn to **156**.

160

Trying not to look down, you advance along the perilous walkway. Sulsa Doom waits for you with his heavy black swords raised.

SULSA DOOM   VIGOUR 15

Roll two dice:
score 2 to 3   You take two wounds; lose 6 VIGOUR
score 4 to 6   You are hit once and lose 3 VIGOUR
score 7 to 12   Sulsa Doom loses 3 VIGOUR

If you win, turn to **260**. If you wish to FLEE by diving into the shaft, throw the dice as usual and then turn to **227**.

161

You open the urn and invert it over the smoking form of the dead Phoenix. Cold black cinders pour out and soon cover the body in an ashen blanket that prevents it from catching alight.

You are on the point of leaving when you notice one of the Phoenix's flame-coloured feathers lying nearby — one of the many it lost during your ferocious fight. You can take a feather if you wish (remember to note it down on your Character Sheet). Will you now go east along the tunnel under the balcony (turn to **91**), or ascend the other staircase (turn to **16**)?

162

You activate the ring just in time. A stream of incandescent white flame passes harmlessly through your body as the power of the ring turns you insubstantial for a few seconds. You become solid once more. The ring crumbles into corroded fragments now that its magic has been expended. You must act quickly now, before the dragon can unleash another jet of fire.

Will you fight it with your sword (turn to **182**), or use one of the items you have collected (turn to **148**)?

You pass through a succession of high peaked chambers. A long cloistered gallery runs parallel to these and, although your eyes cannot penetrate the utter darkness beyond the pillars, you gradually become convinced that something is moving along the gallery, keeping pace with you as you go from room to room. A slight noise so alarms Minki that he scrambles up your cloak to perch on your shoulder. You wait for more than a minute — tense, standing perfectly still, staring into the black arches of the gallery. You can see nothing there.

Finally you accept that your mind is starting to play tricks on you. However, just as you are about to continue on your way, another sound echoes out of the darkness. Minki is so panicky by now that he jumps right up on to the top of your head and holds on tight by grabbing your ears! You gently lift him off. As your fingers encircle his tiny frame, you can feel the pounding of his heart. Or is it your own pulse? Turn to **185**.

You retreat into the cool, ink-black shadows beside the great stairway and press yourself back into a niche in the stone. A minute or so later, the two men draw level with your hiding place. You had believed you were the first to rediscover the pyramid so you are shocked to discover two armed and armoured warriors patrolling it. You are still more shocked when you hear their voices and realize they are from your own land. But all becomes sickeningly clear when one of them half turns and you recognize the black-and-white crest on his surcoat, for it marks him as one of Damontir's men. Somehow your hated foe has beaten you to the temple, perhaps by a margin of only hours or minutes. They stop to swig rough gin from a hipflask, and you take the opportunity to eavesdrop on what they are saying.

'Blow this for a lark,' growls one, slapping away a fly that was feasting on his beefy neck. 'I can take the boredom and the heat, but these insects are goin' ter drink me dry before the boss gets back. Why didn't 'e take us wiv him, I want ter know.'

'Yer great lemon!' His companion spits on the baked earth. 'Yer better off out 'ere, ent yer? Want ter go wanderin' around an old tomb wiv a nutjob like Damontir? Never come out again, would yer?'

'Temple,' replied the first, gargling his gin before swallowing it.

'Yer what?'

'It's not a tomb, it's a temple. I heard the guv'nor say.'

The second man snorts. 'Temple, tomb, where's the difference? Damontir wouldn't trust the likes of us wiv all that treasure around, would 'e? That's what 'e's got them freaks — whassit, Nightmare Guards — for, innit?'

You have heard enough. If Damontir is here with his fearsome Nightmare Guard then you have no time to waste. Will you attack the two men (turn to **70**) or will you try to scale the steps to the top without them noticing (turn to **184**)?

165

The last native battles on, but you have wiped the vicious smile from his face now!

Roll two dice:
score 2 to 3	You are hit and lose 3 VIGOUR
score 4 to 12	Your adversary loses 3 VIGOUR

If you win, turn to **61**.

166

Minki shrieks and chatters and cavorts along the balustrade, elated at your victory. A sulphurous tang assaults your nostrils. The robe at your feet is crumpling into shapeless folds and a thick yellow vapour wafts from it as the body within disintegrates. The fate of all the Nightmare Guard when slain is to return to the smouldering ashes from which they were created.

You lift the creature's garrotte from where it lies. It is only a scarf of midnight blue silk decorated with a pattern of white skulls — a thing seemingly harmless, even if in questionable taste. Yet in the expert hands of the Nightmare Guard it became a lethal weapon which almost robbed you of your life. You drop it by the limp black robe and, gathering up Minki on your shoulder, descend a staircase at one end of the balcony to the floor of the great hall. You move along past the screened brazier, your own shadow sharp against the diffuse bars of light and shade, towards a pair of doors in the centre of the east wall below the balcony. The doors are heavy blocks of mahogany, inlaid with sculpted panels of smooth coral. There is no other way out of the hall, so you pull them open and step through. Turn to **136**.

167

You swing the door open and peer into the chamber beyond. A few footprints mark the dust near the doorway, but Damontir seems not to have gone any further into the room. The white stone reflects your sword's light starkly. A huge golden flame-symbol dominates the opposite wall. Below this there is a marble slab on which lies a sparkling pendant. You may either cross the room and examine the pendant (turn to **37**) or close the door and continue west (turn to **269**).

168

You cannot stand; you think you may have broken your leg. Writhing white flames form a high barrier all around, and you look up to see a slender figure silhouetted against them. You struggle to rise as Damontir approaches, but it is no use.

'Ah, Dragon Knight,' he murmurs, standing over you, 'how fitting that you should grovel on the floor at my feet.'

The Ring of Red Ruin sparkles as Damontir brings up his arm. He gloats, knowing you cannot avoid the blast. Your life ends in a searing flare of magical energy.

169

With Minki fleeing like the wind ahead of you, you race back into the antechamber. The creature lopes awkwardly in pursuit, its huge eye bobbing as it tries to take aim for the blast that will end your life. You are directly between the creature and the tapestry-draped wall. You turn to face it. The single eye shines like the sun, bloated with energy. You are sure it is about to fire, and you hurl yourself aside with a speed born of desperation.

Roll two dice, trying to score equal to or less than your *current* AGILITY. If you succeed, turn to **262**. If you fail, turn to **287**.

170

Cool air gusts out as you swing the doors open — a welcome contrast to the humid warmth of the dragon's lair. You enter a large room with a low level ceiling that is unsupported by beams or pillars. Ripples of pale blue light wash across the grey stone, reflected from a pool which runs the length of the room. Steps lead down into the pool, which does not appear to be very deep. At the far end of the room squats a large, reddish-black statue with fire opals for eyes. As you approach the statue, you see that its hands are folded in its lap and cupped to hold an ebony drum.

If you wish to step up to the statue and take the drum, turn to **144**. Otherwise you could investigate the pool (turn to **49**) or else leave this room and head west along the corridor (turn to **119**).

You reach out your hand...
Turn to **259**.

You slip the ring on to your finger. It is a magic Ring of Healing. You may use this *once* during your adventure, at any time except during a battle. It will immediately restore your VIGOUR to its *normal* level. Remember that there is only enough magic in the Ring of Healing for one use, so you must choose the moment carefully. Taking a deep breath, you head back along the tunnel to the main corridor and make your way south.
Turn to **194**.

The crude trail ends at a small clearing, beyond which the trees cluster thickly once more. In the middle of the clearing you see a small, lichen stained stone figurine lying on the matted grass. If you wish to inspect the stone figurine, turn to **23**. If you would rather ignore it and press on, turn to **5**.

Disappointingly, you experience no surge of strength as you fasten the belt around your waist. Perhaps it has magical properties that will become obvious later. If you have not already done so, you may now take the ring (turn to **45**) or the bottle of blue liquid (turn to **6**). If you are ready to leave, turn to **240**.

You will need to be fleet of foot to outdistance the hurtling boulder. Roll two dice. If the total is less than or equal to your *current* AGILITY score, turn to **132**. If the total is greater than your AGILITY then the boulder catches up with you — turn to **46**.

176

If you have a Phoenix feather, turn to **47**. If not, turn to **245**.

177

As you drink from the chalice, you feel it draining your reserves of psychic strength. Lose 1 point of PSI. With a cry of bitter rage, you hurl it from you and watch it skid across the floor into the shadows. Was it, then, only a baneful lure? A sadistic jest played upon you by men who died long ages past? Cursing the depletion of your PSI, you head west out of the room.

Turn to **87**.

178

If you were stung by the scorpion, turn to **26**. If you managed to defeat it without being stung even once, you now scramble up out of the pit and leave through the door in the north wall (turn to **152**).

179

As you reach for the drum, brilliant rays lance from the statue's opal eyes. Suddenly flames spurt up around you. You start back, but your mounting panic changes to bewildered amazement when you realize that the flames are not burning you. Within moments they dwindle and die. You are left unmarked, completely unharmed! Obviously some sorcery in the water of the pool protected you. Quickly, before the defensive magic can wear off, you step up to the statue. However, now that you are this close, you notice something — its arms are pivoted at the shoulders. They are doubtless counterweighted, and if you remove the drum they will swing upwards and activate some hidden mechanism. In order to avoid this, you consider substituting another item in its place. If you wish to do this, decide which item you will use and turn to **67**. If you are not prepared to relinquish any of the items you have collected, you could just take the drum and risk setting off a trap (turn to **195**), or you could leave this room without the drum and head west (turn to **119**).

180

Your curiosity is aroused by a granite monolith, carved to depict a squat demon with a grinning death's-head, holding a plaque in its clawed hands. You step up on to the circular dais in front of the monolith to examine this plaque more closely. Most of the glyphs that scar the crumbling stone are indecipherable, their meaning lost in antiquity, but the five symbols which dominate the centre of the plaque are clear to you. They represent the principal deities of the Anku Empire. A jagged line corresponds to the thunder-god Tlal. Tonu the sun-god is shown as a disc fringed with radial lines. The large stylized flame in the middle is dearly the emblem of Katak himself. The open outline of a skull denotes Ictec, the god of the netherworld. And the last glyph, a short spiral, represents the Anku deity of arts and crafts, whose name is now forgotten. In some mysterious way you feel compelled to touch one of these glyphs — but which:

The jagged line?	Turn to **259**
The sun-disc?	Turn to **143**
The stylized flame?	Turn to **222**
The skull symbol?	Turn to **171**
The spiral?	Turn to **281**

You fancy you hear a faint howl as one of the spectral warriors dissolves into dust and scattered light. The others fight on without a sound.

Roll two dice:

score 2 to 3	You are hit twice, lose 6 VIGOUR
score 4 to 5	You are hit once; lose 3 VIGOUR
score 6 to 12	One of the spectral warriors (you choose which) loses 3 VIGOUR

You have the opportunity to FLEE now by retreating the way you came. If you do that, turn to **250** (remember that they will *both* try to hit you as you run so you must throw the dice twice).

If you fight on and destroy another, turn to **202**.

182

Even an enchanted sword like yours seems a puny weapon against so massive and powerful a creature – but you have no other choice.

RED DRAGON   VIGOUR 18

Roll two dice:

score 2 to 7	You are wounded, lose 4 VIGOUR
score 8 to 12	The dragon loses 3 VIGOUR

You cannot get past it to FLEE. If you kill it, turn to **159**.

183

The revenant was an accomplished magician in life, and you are unable to resist the powerful spell it has cast upon you. Through the sensation of numbing cold, you feel something stirring within your body. You drop your sword and stare in horror as green tendrils erupt from your skin and twist around you. As the magical creepers choke the life from you, the last thing you see is the grisly rictus of your foe as it tears the jewelled pectoral from your chest.

184

You are barely halfway up in your steep climb when a shout rings out from below. You have been spotted. As the two sentries ready their crossbows, you race up towards the summit. You are almost there when they level their bows and shoot.

Roll one die:

score 1	Turn to **149**
score 2 or 3	Both quarrels hit you; lose 6 VIGOUR
score 4 or 5	Only one hits you; lose 3 VIGOUR
score 6	They both miss you

If you are still alive, you stagger up the remaining few steps and on to the flat top of the pyramid out of the sentries' line of sight. Turn to **102**.

185

You leave Minki in the middle of the room and advance slowly towards the cloistered gallery, holding your sword ahead to drive back the shadows. Suddenly there is a ghastly shriek and a staring, green-tinted skeleton rushes out of the darkness, flailing at you with its cracked fingers. The Anku nobleman has come to reclaim what you stole from his grave.

REVENANT	VIGOUR 9

Roll two dice:

score 2 to 6	You are wounded; lose 3 VIGOUR
score 7 to 12	The revenant loses 3 VIGOUR

You cannot FLEE — if you do not destroy the creature now it will pursue you forever. If the revenant wounds you on two *consecutive* dice rolls, turn to **151**. If you manage to defeat it without it ever hitting you twice in a row, turn to **286**.

186

Wraith-like figures that seem to have arisen from an awful nightmare drift and recede in the thick smoke. Their icy insubstantial touch drains your very soul. Lose 3 PSI points. Your nerve breaks and you scream again and again as you run down the fog-shrouded stairs. You cannot see clearly where to tread, and suddenly your foot slips on the edge of a step and you start to fall forwards. Try to roll your current AGILITY or less on two dice. If you succeed, turn to **291**. If you fail, turn to **115**.

187

You hurry back along the tunnel before the great bird can resurrect itself once more. Crossing the coruscating floor, you hurriedly ascend the other stairway. Turn to **16**.

188

Giving your captors no time to react, you lunge forward and rip your sword from the startled native's grasp. Two of the natives dart forward to seize you. You cut them down with a single stroke. Blood sprays across the faces of the witchdoctor and his chief warriors and, as they flinch back, you make good your escape. Turn to **189**.

189

You race to the edge of the clearing and into the waiting jungle. The natives are not slow to give chase. You plunge on through a sea of sharp dark leaves that cut you like spikes of volcanic glass. Fortunately, although the natives know the jungle rather better than you do, they continually give away their position with their shouts and hunting cries. Eventually you manage to slip right between their front runners and the main search party and leave them far behind as you make your way roughly north-west. You think the Temple of Katak must lie somewhere ahead of you.

Roll one die. If you score 1-3, turn to **18**. If you score 4-6, turn to **246**.

190

You walk along the corridor and emerge on to a high balcony overlooking a large hall. Carved panels on the walls depict ceremonies of devotion to the flame-god Katak. Looking down to the floor of the hall, you see six fretwork screens of gleaming silver placed in a hexagon about a crackling brazier. The leaping flame spreads a cobweb of shadows from the screens right out across the hall. Within the area enclosed by the screens, the firelight is thrown back in bright reticular patterns of great beauty. How extraordinary it is to stand here and gaze upon this work of the Anku priest-lords, this living art that has outlived the civilization that created it by more than two thousand years!

You are so absorbed in admiration of the ancient artefacts and carvings that you do not notice a black-clad form drop from the lintel of the archway behind you. It is one of the Nightmare Guard, Damontir's retinue of unhuman assassins. As it stalks towards you, Minki suddenly utters a shrill cry and skitters away nervously. His warning gives you

just enough time to whirl and strike at the oncoming assailant with your sword. It falls back for an instant, then lunges at you again, anxious to encircle your neck with its garrotte of weighted silk.

NIGHTMARE GUARD   VIGOUR 12

Roll two dice:
score 2 to 5   Turn to **63**
score 6 to 12   Your opponent loses 3 VIGOUR

If you kill it, turn to **166**. If you try to FLEE down the steps from the balcony, do not roll the dice as you would normally do, but turn to **75**.

191

Something hard clamps around your shins. You look down to discover that your legs are shackled with glowing chains, icy cold and green as emerald. You seize them and twist and strain at the links, but all your strength is not enough to break them. These are magical chains which the pendant has created in your own mind — you cannot shatter them, nor sever them with your sword's keen blade. Damontir left the pendant as bait for you, having first placed a curse upon it, in case your battle with Sulsa Doom did not have the outcome he hoped for. Reduce your *current* AGILITY score to 3 because of the chains. (If your AGILITY is *already* 3 or less, reduce it by 1 point.)

Furious with yourself for succumbing to Damontir's ploy, you shuffle from the room and head west once more.

Turn to **269**.

192

Although single-minded in their defence of the temple, the undead Skullghasts are not able to truly think and reason. They recognize the pectoral and, believing you to be a noble of the ancient Anku Empire, break off the attack and return to their niches. You breathe a sigh of relief at your narrow escape and depart through the opening in the western wall. Turn to **163**.

193

After discarding your old cloak, you take the cloak of feathers down from where it hangs and drape it across your shoulders. As you turn to leave the room you see that Minki has become quite agitated, darting to and fro as he utters long wailing cries. You soon see the cause of his alarm — the serpentine pillars are slowly uncoiling. There is the sound of stone grinding against stone as the huge creatures move to block your exit. You tighten your grip on your sword and prepare to give battle.

First STONE SERPENT   VIGOUR 12

Roll two dice:
score 2 to 5   You are wounded; lose 3 VIGOUR
score 6 to 12   The serpent loses 3 VIGOUR

If you win, turn to **237**.

194

After a while the corridor you are in is joined by another leading east. Will you take the new corridor (turn to **205**) or continue walking south (turn to **8**)?

195

At first nothing happens when you lift the drum from the statue's lap. You see now that a decorative motif runs around it — angular carvings showing warriors with their bodies twisted in the lusty barbaric war-dance of the Anku Empire. You are just fastening the straps of your backpack, having put the drum inside it, when the massive arms of the statue begin to pivot up. You hear the creak of chains and weights behind the walls and start to hurry towards the exit, ready to break into a run at the first indication of danger. The mechanism you have set in motion, however, is not a trap at all. Instead, one of the blocks forming the eastern wall descends slowly into the floor to reveal a passage. If you wish to leave the room by this new route, turn to **298**. If you would rather return to the vestibule and take the corridor heading west, turn to **119**.

196
The native spear buries itself in your chest, bringing your adventure to an abrupt and bloody conclusion.

197
Sweat beads your brow and your arms are trembling with the strain when you finally reach the top and haul yourself over on to the floor of the chamber. Your sword lies on the plinth and you must retrieve it before going on — not only is it your main weapon, it is also your only light source. You jump back across on to the plinth, wincing at the pain from your injured ankle. The black vapour has dispersed into nebulous wisps by now. You lift your sword so that its glow illuminates the interior of the open casket. There you see a bronze ring, a wide belt studded with polished opals and a quartz bottle containing a blue liquid. If you wish to leave all of these where they are, turn to **240**. If not, which item will you take first:

The belt?	Turn to **174**
The ring?	Turn to **45**
The bottle?	Turn to **6**

198
The battle ends with the golem victorious, standing like a colossus amid the broken and twisted bodies of the cadavers. It is not undamaged — the cadavers' rain of blows cleaved great sheets of stone from its body, and one hand has been shattered at the wrist. As its dull eyes fall upon you it begins to move haltingly forward. Will you fight it (turn to **265**) or avoid combat by running south (turn to **72**)?

199

You make your way along a wide, low-ceilinged corridor, past basalt stonework inlaid with abstract patterns in red and grey marble. As your sword-light dispels the darkness, you see that the corridor veers sharply left some distance ahead of you. Suddenly, with a loud scraping sound, a stone slab begins to descend from the roof of the corridor in front of you. A quick backward glance tells you there is no retreat — another slab is sliding down to block the corridor behind you. Within moments, the section of corridor in which you stand will be completely sealed off. If you wish to run forward and try to get under the slab before it reaches the floor, turn to **128**. If you would rather stand where you are and see what happens, turn to **34**.

200

Your climb to the summit is not nearly so arduous as you had expected. Although a shimmering haze of heat rises from the dark basalt steps, there is a steady breeze which seems refreshingly cool after your trek through the steaming jungle. The sun burns relentlessly down, throwing elaborate shadows across the grotesque carvings which leer at intervals from the sides of the stairway. These stone faces are fanciful representations of Katak's sixteen Celestial Emissaries, once venerated as demigods. Ignorant of this, little Minki capers irreverently over them as the two of you ascend the steps. As you near the top, you pause and turn to stare out across the trackless verdant expanse. You cannot see the river itself from here, but you can just make out the sparkling tip of the crystal spire next to which your ship lies at anchor. Minki tugs at your boot, hopping from one foot to the other on the oven-hot stone as if to tell you that he does not appreciate the delay. Chuckling, you mount the last few steps to the pyramid's flat top.

Turn to **102**.

201

As the creature dies, the lines of its form shift and alter. You are standing over the dead body of the witchdoctor. Did you truly fight a demon, or was it merely an illusion that the old man conjured? The truth remains forever unknowable. You expect the warriors of the tribe to fall upon you at any moment, to bring you down with sheer weight of numbers. You are prepared to sell your life dearly, but when you turn to face them you see that there will be no need for that. The entire village is bowing down to you, overawed by your defeat of their witchdoctor. One of them crawls forward and offers you the witchdoctor's bone wand. You take it (remember to note it down on your Character Sheet), but you have no intention of assuming his position in the tribe if that is what is meant by the gesture.

As you turn to leave, you are pleased to see Minki waiting for you by the edge of the village. As the natives cower and moan, you head off into the jungle. Turn to **80**.

202

The last of the three lunges at you with its ethereal sword. On the sombre, dusty mask of its dead features no flicker of expression shows.

Roll two dice:
score 2 to 3   You are hit; lose 3 VIGOUR
score 4 to 12   The spectral warrior loses 3 VIGOUR

If you FLEE back the way you came, turn to **250**. If you destroy your ghostly foe, turn to **106**.

203

The cloak stirs in the rushing air and spreads to form a resplendent canopy across your back. Your rate of descent slows to a gentle glide as you spiral down the shaft to land safely on a rock in the middle of the lake. The cloak immediately moults, falling away in a shower of magnificently coloured plumage. Its magic saved your life, but it was usable only once. All around you lie the seething waters of the lake. Rock outcroppings jut up at intervals out of the bubbling surface. Through the shimmer of heat and rising steam you can see a black archway in the north wall of the shaft. You start to make your way towards this by jumping from rock to rock, using them as stepping stones. Turn to **275**.

204

You dive back out of the way and the bolt hits the floor where you were standing. A thin wisp of vaporized stone curls up from where it struck. Turn to **242**.

205

Reaching the end of the corridor, you walk up a ramp paved with translucent rose-tinted onyx and find yourself in a funerary chamber. Four embalmed warriors dressed in their gilded and plumed battle finery stand in alcoves, silent sentinels of the past. Seeing a passage in the extreme end of the south wall, you step off the ramp towards it. At the very moment you do so, your worst fears are realized — a reddish glow arises within the alcoves, limning their occupants eerily, and then the dead warriors stir! As they lurch towards you, you raise your sword. Its cold light illuminates the lustreless ashen skin, the pupil-less eyes like antique ivory. Their movements are awkward and faltering at first, but gradually acquire energy, fluidity — even a certain nightmarish grace.

Perhaps there is an item in your backpack you might use against them? If so, turn to **20**. If not, you must fight: turn to **41**.

206

The remaining skullghasts abandon the attack and float back up to their niches. You are left standing amid the shattered shards of bone, some still flickering with occult flame. In the aftermath of the harrowing battle you find

yourself trembling uncontrollably. It is only when you see Minki's familiar face peering quizzically up at you that you regain your composure enough to continue onwards. Turn to **53**.

207

You find yourself in a narrow chamber. There is another flight of steps leading up, but you are more interested in the wide spiral staircase in the middle of the room. You look down, but can see only darkness below. Sure that this is the correct route to your goal, you begin to descend the spiral staircase. You notice tendrils of smoke curling around your ankles. A thick, filmy haze hangs in the air, and as you go on it seems that you are walking down through curtains of black lace. The darkness closes in around you. Coughing, you stumble on although you can barely see the steps through the dense smoke. Faint moans and cries of terror and anguish drift half-heard to your ears, as though from an unimaginable distance. Within the veils of smoke you catch brief glimpses of shapes and faces which chill your blood. If you have a conch shell trumpet, turn to **244**. If you do not have this item, turn to **85**.

208

The tunnel is joined by a number of side passages, but you follow Damontir's footprints steadily north and finally emerge into another chamber. Turn to **145**.

209

You stop short and your hand goes to your sword as two natives step out on to the path ahead of you. Grotesque tattoos cover their faces and their teeth are filed to gleaming points. You back away and start to turn — there is a third native behind you. Your sword blade flashes in the afternoon sunlight as they circle to attack you with their long spears. Turn to **117**.

210

After a while the corridor you are in joins a second corridor running east and west. You decide to take the western branch. Turn to **190**.

211

Through thick clouds of dust thrown up by the boulder's passing, your shining sword illuminates a passage leading west. There is another corridor to the south, but that is now blocked by the boulder. If you have a Ring of Intangibility and wish to use it, you could go south (turn to **64**). Otherwise you must head west (turn to **290**).

212

You throw yourself through the closing gap and just manage to scramble out of the way as the slab comes down on the stone floor with a dull crunch. You get up and brush the dust from your tunic and armour. You can only stare at the heavy slab that now blocks the corridor — a fraction slower and you would have been entombed behind it, or crushed under it. The priests of Katak jealously guarded their shrine with numerous fiendish traps. This will certainly not have been the last of them, and you must remain alert. Turning the corner, you proceed west until you enter another corridor. Damontir has left his footprints in the dust here. You follow them northwards into a large chamber.

Did you succumb to the priest-kings' curse? If so, turn to **279**. If not, turn to **145**.

213

You head west and finally emerge into a room with small dark niches high up in the walls. A stark white skull rests in each. There is a marble pedestal at one end of the room. Stylized flames are carved around its base and a large red gem lies on the floor beside it. If you wish to pick up the gem, turn to **62**. If you wish to cross the room and leave by the passage in the opposite wall, turn to **53**.

214

You start to notice the stifling heat in the tunnel when you are nearing the steps at the western end. Your breathing is shallow and laborious — you cannot seem to draw any air into your lungs. Will you turn back (turn to **123**), or hurry along to the steps at the end (turn to **230**)?

215

Glancing around for a nearby rock to leap to, you delay a moment too long. The world disappears in an incandescent white blaze as the dragon's fiery breath engulfs you. Lose 12 VIGOUR points. If you survive this, the flame subsides and you frantically brush at your tunic where it has caught alight.

You must act quickly now, before the dragon has a chance to breathe again. Will you fight it with your sword (turn to **182**), or will you use one of the items you have collected (turn to **148**)?

216

Your final spear-thrust pierces the sentry's heart and he sinks to the floor as his blood washes over the ancient stones. You may keep the spear if you wish — note it down on your Character Sheet if so. You look around the ruins for ways down into the pyramid. One seems almost too obvious — a heavy flagstone with a metal ring in the middle, set into the stone floor. You can see from the dirt and moss caking the fine cracks around it that the flagstone has not been lifted up for years, perhaps centuries. Damontir found some other route down.

You glance up as the sky rumbles. Thunderclouds are piling up like slate on the distant horizon. As they slide in from the north, a mist of rain hides the far-off mountain peaks. The storm advances swiftly, and the first drops of rain are already spattering the basalt steps as you return to the problem of how you are going to enter the pyramid.

If you wish to lift the flagstone and descend that way, turn to **36**. If you intend to search for another entrance, turn to **180**.

217

You finally reach a corridor running north-south. Will you go north (turn to **210**) or south (turn to **24**)?

218

You find yourself in a plain, rubble-strewn gallery which you have entered at the northern end. You notice another door nearby, but decide to head south. As you do so, a massive figure which in the gloom you mistook for a statue stirs and lumbers across the room. It is a great golem with a body of unyielding slate. Although surprised, you continue to beat the drum. Your cadavers stalk forward and fall upon the golem with ghastly voiceless battle-cries. They are lithe, and press their attack with unthinking savagery, inexorably chipping away at the golem with their jagged weapons. But the stony creature retaliates by flailing its great arms about, and at each blow that connects you hear the snap of ancient bones.

If you wish, you may cast down the drum and head south along the gallery (turn to **72**). If you would rather stay and see the outcome of the fight, turn to **198**.

219

A jewelled barge glides from one of the dark arches around the walls and drifts towards you trailing a slowly undulating wake. A robed figure stands like a tall orange flame in the prow. As the barge draws near, the figure's cowl falls back from its face and your sword-light gleams on lustrous metal. It is a gold-plated skeleton, holding out its hand to receive some gift or payment. You know well what it requires from you. You drop the black pearl into its latticed palm and step down into the barge. Propelled by some sorcerous means, the vessel slowly turns and you are conveyed eerily across to the pyramid steps. Turn to **270**.

220

You race along the tunnel for only a short distance and then skid to a halt. It is a dead end. The Phoenix, knowing this, has given chase. You turn to find it almost upon you.

PHOENIX   VIGOUR 12

Roll two dice:
score 2 to 6   You are hit; lose 3 VIGOUR
score 7 to 12   The Phoenix loses 3 VIGOUR

You cannot get past it to FLEE — this battle is to the death. If you win, turn to **187**.

221

The mouldering threads of the tapestry rot and shred away like cobwebs at your touch, leaving you staring straight into the eyes of a grim-faced warrior with a glowing sword. You jump back startled, but it is only your own reflection in a huge mirror. You find it odd that the shimmering surface of the mirror has not deteriorated in so many years. Perhaps the priests of Katak placed some preservative enchantments upon it. You laugh as you notice Minki glowering at his own reflection and lift him up on to your shoulder before leaving the room and heading north. Turn to **277**.

Katak's own glyph is the logical choice, since this is his temple. As your finger traces the weathered grooves, there is a groan of chains and gears from below and then the circular dais on which you are standing begins to descend into the pyramid. Minki leaps hastily to join you as the dais drops away, and the two of you are conveyed down into darkness...

Turn to **154**.

Shortly after turning to the right, the corridor ends at a junction. Seeing that Damontir's footprints head west from here, you decide to follow them. Turn to **12**.

Writhing white flames form an impassable barrier all around. Ahead of you, Damontir stands alone amid the empty robes of the remaining Nightmare Guard. They died battling a massive six-limbed monster of jade and steel that now lies broken and still. It must have guarded this cavern through aeons, the last guardian of the sacred idol. Its battle against the Nightmare Guard has been fearsome and closely matched. Even Damontir, who is usually one to hold back from personal danger, is cut and bloodied. You stare at him with seething hatred as you approach. His cloak hangs about him, giving him the appearance of a foul, white plumed scavenger bird as he pours over the ancient runes carved on a granite podium.

He notices you and turns, saying, 'Ah! You got past Sulsa Doom, then. I had a feeling you might.' He gestures at the inscribed podium. 'There is some complex formula for lowering the flames that surround us. The idol lies beyond them, naturally. I should be able to decipher the runes quite quickly, though I daresay you would have no more comprehension of such things than the annoying little monkey I slew earlier.'

You search for phrases to curse this obscenely smirking villain, but can think of none. 'Damontir,' you say flatly. 'You will die by my sword.'

He looks at you sharply, then laughs without mirth. 'Dragon Knight of Palados! Were we to cross blades, perhaps you might be the victor. But I have a dozen sorcerous ways to kill you before you reach me.' He draws something from his tunic. Light flashes across your face as he turns it towards you. 'The Mirror of the Moon.'

Damontir carefully angles the mirror to reflect your own gaze back at you and then releases it. Instead of falling to shatter on the hard stone floor, it floats in mid-air. It starts slowly to rotate, growing larger as it does so until it seems a swirling pool of quicksilver filled by your image. Then, as you stare in stunned incredulity, your own reflection steps out of the mirror and stands before you. Illuminated by the unearthly half-light of its mirror world, it does not quite seem to be your twin. Rather, it looks like a vivid portrait of yourself rendered in unnatural hues.

'This is your Simulacrum,' explains Damontir. 'A soulless duplicate of yourself.' The Simulacrum utters an unreal cry and advances on you with a look of wild malice. 'It is an unreasoning automaton, quite dedicated to its single purpose. Killing you.'

Contemptuously, he turns away from the fight and resumes his translation of the runes on the podium. The Simulacrum has the same VIGOUR as you have at the moment. It is like you in every respect, except that it has neither soul nor intellect, and does not cast a shadow. You prepare yourself for battle.

Turn to **43**.

225

As you drink from the chalice, it automatically casts a healing spell upon you. Increase your *current* VIGOUR by 6 points — unless this would take your VIGOUR above its *normal* score, in which case any excess points are lost. This healing spell draws on your own innate psychic reserves — reduce your PSI by 1 point for the time being. You may keep the chalice and use it anytime as long as you have water to pour into it. Each time you drink you will gain 6 VIGOUR points and lose 1 PSI point; you may do this at any point in your adventure except when you are in combat. You must not use it if that would reduce your PSI score below 2, however. After putting the chalice into your backpack you head west out of the room. Turn to **87**.

226

Sparks of magical radiance jump from the revenant's hands towards you. As they sink into your flesh you feel a bitter chill as though you had been buried in a snowdrift. Roll two dice. If the score is less than or equal to your current PSI, turn to **278**. If greater, turn to **183**.

227

You plunge like an arrow through the rolling mist. A break in the cloud shows you water at the bottom of the shaft — but your relief soon changes to a nausea of fear when you see how the surface of the water bubbles and seethes. You are diving towards a simmering underground lake that must be close to boiling point! Are you wearing a cloak of feathers? If so, turn to **203**. If you have not picked up this item on your quest, turn to **112**.

228

One of the quarrels punctures your lung. You crash to the dusty ground. Shouts and disjointed images swirl about you. Minki is tugging at your cloak with his tiny paws. You are aware of the taste of blood and the dry earth in your mouth. A booted foot turns you over on your back and you claw feebly at it. Someone stands over you, a red shadow against the dazzling sun, and then you pass out. You will never awaken.

229

Twenty centuries ago, the vapour was a volatile toxin that would kill a victim in seconds. You are indeed fortunate that it has oxidized and degenerated over the years. It is now no more than a mild irritant that causes your eyes to water. As the cloud of vapour disperses, you see three items inside the open casket — a bronze ring, a bottle of blue liquid and a belt adorned with polished stones. If you wish to leave these where they are, turn to **240**. If you wish to take any of the items, which will you remove from the casket first:

The belt?	Turn to **174**
The ring?	Turn to **45**
The bottle?	Turn to **6**

230

You ascend the short flight of steps into a large hexagonal room. The air here, although stale and musty, is at least breathable. Feeling slightly faint, you kneel down beside the steps to get your breath back. Scanning the room at leisure, you are most interested in a large suit of bronze armour that stands in an alcove on the other side of the room. As you look at the overlapping plates of burnished metal, engraved with mysterious sigils, you realize that it could not have been fashioned for any human warrior. The whole suit must weigh almost half a tonne! This thought makes you uneasy, and you quickly get to your feet.

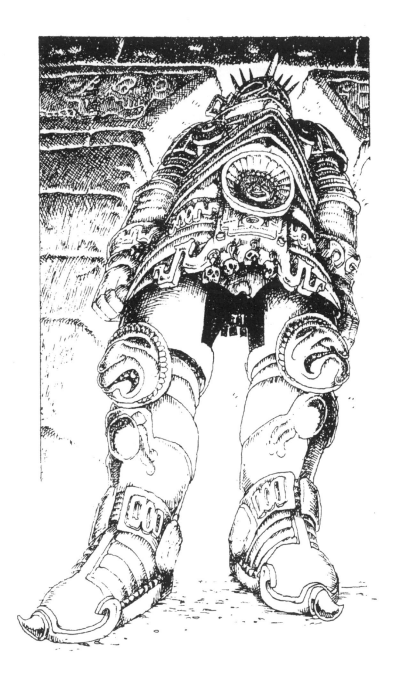

In the wall close by you there is a circular bronze plug with the sacred flame-glyph of Katak embossed upon it. The wall around the plug is livid and scarred, like fused brimstone. If you wish to try removing the plug from the wall, turn to **158**. If you would rather walk back along the tunnel to the main corridor and head south, turn to **194**.

231

Do you have a Ring of Intangibility? If so, turn to 162. If not, you must try to dodge the dragon's breath — try to roll equal to or less than your *current* AGILITY on two dice. If you succeed, turn to **94**. If you fail, turn to **215**.

232

You step up to another of the mummies and shred away the gold leaf to expose another gauntly grinning face. This one, however, holds a black pearl between its yellowed teeth. Damontir obviously felt it worthwhile to take some of these pearls from the corpses of the priest-kings. You reach out and seize the pearl, pulling it from the mummy's jaws with some effort. Note the pearl on your Character Sheet.

As you turn to continue on your way, a sense of stark malevolence looms in upon you like a demon's shadow. It is the curse of the priest-kings, an ancient hex that assails all who desecrate their engilded bodies. In the twenty centuries that have passed since it was laid, however, the curse had lost much of its potency. You need only roll your current PSI or less on *one* die to resist it. If you succeed, turn to **33**. If you fail, turn to **38**.

233

You point at the jars inside the hut and motion for the two nearest warriors to fetch them. Sullenly, they bring the heavy jars outside. Peering within, you find a frothy brew of fermenting juices. This concoction is prepared for ritual use; normally the natives would drink it only at certain sacred festivals, but they break with tradition in view of their Witchdoctor's plight. Still glowering at you, they gulp back the brew in huge quantities and are soon lolling on the ground, helplessly drunk. The witchdoctor himself cantankerously refuses to touch the brew. You do not wish to hurt the old fellow, so you take away his bone wand and medicine pouch to prevent him casting any spells and then tie him up. He watches you in silence, resenting the ignominious treatment but aware that you are an honourable foe. If you decide to keep his wand and pouch, remember to note them on your Character Sheet.

As you turn to leave, you are pleased to find Minki waiting for you by the side of the clearing. By the time the dozing natives sober up, the pair of you will be long gone. You head off into the jungle. Turn to **80**.

234

The priests of Katak created the undead skullghasts to protect their temple from intruders. Having only rudimentary intelligence, the skullghast assumes from the pectoral you wear that you are a noble of the Anku Empire and therefore entitled to walk in the sacred precincts. It hovers before you for a few moments and then settles down on to the pedestal once more. Slightly unnerved by your narrow escape, you back slowly out of the room and try the other door. Turn to **150**.

235

You hurtle through the door and slam it shut behind you. Finding yourself in another corridor, you decide to head west. Turn to **89**.

236

With Minki perched on your shoulder, you walk across to the gallery. You hold your sword up to drive back the gossamer shadows. In the gloom beyond the pillars you can dimly make out a line of statues along the gallery, so badly cracked and worn that they look like victims of leprosy. Something gleams dully in the magical light. You stoop and pick up a small jadeite figurine in the shape of a plummeting eagle. Note this item down on your Character Sheet if you decide to keep it. You turn away from the gallery and head west once more.

Turn to **217**.

237

Even as your first adversary falls in a shower of chipped rock, the second slithers inexorably forward.

Second STONE SERPENT VIGOUR 12

Roll two dice:
score 2 to 5   You are wounded and lose 3 VIGOUR
score 6 to 12   The serpent loses 3 VIGOUR

If you win, turn to **71**.

238

You are now gasping for breath, and it is all you can do to wield your sword with aching arms as you watch your last opponent stalk towards you.

Roll two dice:
score 2 to 5   You lose 3 VIGOUR
score 6 to 12   The cadaver loses 3 VIGOUR

If you FLEE south, turn to **15**. If you defeat the cadaver, turn to **54**.

239

How many times did the scorpion sting you? You must roll higher than this number on one die in order to shrug off the effects of its venom. Roll the die, and if the number you roll exceeds the number of times you were stung, turn to **297**. If not, turn to **99**.

You jump over the deep pit, swing your pack over your shoulder and head west out of the room. Turn to **69**.

As the greatest knight of Palados, you should have little trouble with two scruffy thugs like these!

| FIRST SENTRY | VIGOUR 9 |
| SECOND SENTRY | VIGOUR 9 |

Roll two dice:

score 2 to 3	You are hit twice; lose 6 VIGOUR
score 4 to 5	You are hit once; lose 3 VIGOUR
score 6 to 12	One of the sentries (you choose which) loses 3 VIGOUR

When you have put one of them down, turn to **113**.

You circle warily as Damontir stalks closer, taunting you all the while by waving his deadly ring as though it were the merest bauble. You feel stone behind you — you see that you have backed into the wall next to the alcove. The eternally fierce visage of the idol looks out sightlessly across the cavern. Damontir's ring glows angrily.

'There is nowhere left to run,' he says. 'Goodbye.'

The ruby beam shoots from the ring — and fizzles out in mid-air, inches from your face! Damontir could not be any more astonished than you are. A host of feelings show on his thin face — surprise, disbelief, thwarted rage. Fear.

Damontir gapes at the idol and then at your broadsword, which you notice shines less brightly now. You have the answer, as he does — the idol must in some way suppress magic within a limited radius. But you cannot stay within the safety of this zone. You must rush the insane warlock while he is still bewildered. With sword raised high you leap towards him. He stares at you in stark terror and raises a shaking hand. He has time for one shot before you close. To dodge this you must roll equal to or less than your current AGILITY on two dice — if you fail, you lose 15 VIGOUR points. (Alternatively, if you have a Ring of Intangibility, you can activate it and allow the flame-bolt to pass harmlessly through you. The ring will crumble after use).

If you survive then you reach Damontir. Turn to **30**.

243

In the days of the Anku Empire, the scions of the nobility customarily entered the priesthood and learned the art of magic. The revenant you are fighting was obviously an adept pupil, for its touch carries a spell that causes motes of green light to erupt from your body. You try to fend it away, but the darting green lights are numbing your limbs and poisoning your blood. As your vision fades, the last thing you see is the twisted grin of the revenant as it rips its jewelled pectoral from your chest.

244

Perhaps some supernatural influence guides you to raise the trumpet to your lips and blow. It produces a deep, low note which builds to a thunderous rumble. You stop blowing, but the noise continues to grow. Suddenly the conch shell bursts asunder and, as it does so, you hear the shriek of a violent gale. Though you feel no wind yourself, you behold its effects — the smoke cloud is thrust back as if a giant invisible hand had swept through it.

The wind soon drops, but by the time it does there are only a few faint wisps of smoke left in the air. The trumpet was an item consecrated to the Anku thunder-god Tlal. When you sounded it, you brought its sacred power against the malevolent smoke wraiths which might otherwise have claimed your soul.

Once the smoke has completely dispersed, you continue down the stairs. Turn to **100**.

245

You fall down a shaft which runs right down through the silver pyramid and opens into a cavern below it. It is difficult to see clearly within the dazzling column of light and, although you are braced for your impact with the floor, you still land awkwardly. Reduce your *current* AGILITY by 2 points. If your AGILITY is now zero, turn to **168**. Otherwise turn to **224**.

246

You press onwards, feeling very much alone until your spirits are lifted by the sight of an old friend swinging through the trees towards you. Minki gambols and frolics around you, beside himself with joy at finding you alive.

Turn to **80**.

247

As the smoke disperses, so do you. The smoke wraiths have claimed you as their own, and you are a part of their shadow world now.

248

You hurl it away from you and the gem splinters against the marble wall. Your lack of caution was very dangerous. The pendant was almost certainly a magical trap left by Damontir in case you survived to pursue him. He would have had one of his Nightmare Guard place it on the slab, of course — that was why there were no footprints across the dusty floor. Resolving to be on your guard from now on, you return to the corridor and head west once more.

Turn to **269**.

249

The black-garbed assassins creep silently towards you. Beneath their veils of grey silk, their crescent eyes flicker like windows on the starry night. You can discern no other feature of the hooded faces. You know that if you tried to escape they would cut you down before you had gone three paces. It is a fight to the death — yours or theirs.

| First NIGHTMARE GUARD | VIGOUR 12 |
| Second NIGHTMARE GUARD | VIGOUR 12 |

Roll two dice:

score 2 to 4	You are hit by both; lose 6 VIGOUR
score 5 to 6	You are hit by one of them; lose 3 VIGOUR
score 7 to 12	One of the Nightmare Guards (you choose which) loses 3 VIGOUR

If you kill one of them, turn to **285**.

250

In the hope of finding a more direct — and less potentially hazardous — route into the heart of the temple, you retrace your steps. You ascend into the ruined building atop the pyramid to find that the storm has broken overhead. Warm rain falls in a staggering deluge and as you look out across the jungle treetops, you find the writhing expanse of green reminiscent of a storm-churned sea. For a moment your thoughts dwell upon your ship and the sailors aboard her. Is your peril in this haunted place any greater than theirs, out there on the seething river with lightning dropping splinters of light into the semi-darkness? As rain lashes the weathered stone, you begin to search for another way down into the pyramid.

Turn to **180**.

251

You have gone only a few paces into the hall when you think you hear a faint noise behind you. Looking back, you can see nothing in the blackness of the corridor along which you have just come. Though anxious to press on, you make your way back to the mouth of the corridor. Blue sword-light rends the velvet dark. A green-tinted skeleton stands before you, spotted with wet grass and grave-mould. Suddenly it screams — a shrill, unearthly sound — and lunges at your throat with its splintered fingers. The Anku nobleman whose grave you rifled has risen from the dead to pursue you.

REVENANT   VIGOUR 9

Roll two dice:
score 2 to 3   Turn to **226**
score 4 to 6   You are wounded; lose 3 VIGOUR
score 7 to 12   The revenant loses 3 VIGOUR

You must not FLEE from this battle — unless you destroy the revenant now, it will hunt you forevermore. If you win, turn to **110**.

252

You pull the sceptre from your belt and brandish it before the dragon — which is, however, wholly unimpressed. Uttering a growl of smoke and flickering fire, it lashes out with scything talons and rakes the sceptre from your grasp. Lose 4 VIGOUR and, if you are still alive, ready your, sword and prepare to do battle! Turn to **182**.

253

You follow the faint track as it twists and turns between the thick, iron-hard tree trunks. Eventually you pause and wipe your brow. You are just about to take a brief rest and share a little water with Minki when you catch sight of something that makes your blood run cold despite the fierce tropical heat. A fleshless skull grins out at you from behind the hanging fronds. There are many more, set all around the path atop wooden poles.

Do you wish to go back and take the other branch of the trail? If so, turn to **95**. If you decide to ignore the grisly warning and press on regardless, turn to **51**.

254

The skullghasts swoop closer as you take out the gem. This is the item they are fighting to protect. Damontir must have removed it from the pedestal when he passed this way ahead of you. You drop the gem to the floor, just as your arch enemy obviously did, and the skullghasts immediately veer away and return to their niches in the wall. With a last look at the sparkling gem, you fetch Minki and continue on your way. Turn to **53**.

255

If the wand is truly imbued with any magical properties, you have no idea how to call them forth. Certainly it has no effect on the undead warriors as they advance towards you. Turn to **41**.

256

The cold steel of your enchanted blade overcomes the Malgash at last. Its flame dies with it, and it disintegrates into black smouldering ashes. You waste no more time here, but turn away from the scene of this titanic battle while soot still hangs in the air. Beyond the north door you find a passage which you decide to follow westwards. Turn to **89**.

257

There is a large rectangular pit at the southern extremity of the room. On a plinth in the middle of the pit, level with the floor of the room, rests a large casket of black wood. There is

barely more than a metre and a half between the edge of the pit and the plinth. You could jump across quite easily, although you find it discomforting that the light from your sword does not reach far enough to show you the bottom of the pit. If you wish to leap on to the plinth, turn to **103**. If you would rather leave the room through the archway in the west wall, turn to **69**.

258

Although you have slain one of their number, the remaining natives attack with renewed ferocity.

> *Roll two dice:*
> score 2 to 3   You are hit twice — lose 6 VIGOUR
> score 4 to 5   You are hit once — lose 3 VIGOUR
> score 6 to 12   One of your foes (your choice) loses 3 VIGOUR

If you kill a second native, turn to **165**.

259

As you stroke your fingertips along the weathered lines of the glyph, there is a sudden shriek of metal gears from under your feet, and then the circular dais on which you are standing shoots up like a piston and slams into the basalt ceiling. Slowly the ingenious mechanism resets itself, lowering the dais back to its original position. Minki runs around the monolith, whining for his lost friend. All that remains of you now is a smear of pulverized bone and mashed sinew. You have failed in your quest to find the lost idol of Katak.

260

Doom sinks down with a ghastly cry as his shadow-life slips from him. For a moment your hand hovers over the black visor of his helmet. Then, despite your curiosity, you stand back from the body. Better not to gaze upon his death-ravaged face. You roll the body off the walkway and watch the clouds of steam swallow it. After a few seconds, a muffled splash drifts up from the depths.

Your thoughts dwell on poor Minki, who in a space of hours you had come to regard as a friend and boon companion. Victory over the undead Sulsa Doom has not slaked your thirst for vengeance. Damontir himself must pay with his lifeblood. There is a grim cast to your features and your eyes are like chips of ice as you cross to the far side of the shaft and pass through the black archway beyond. Turn to **295**.

261

You try rubbing the paste into your skin. It is oily and rapidly absorbed. As it takes effect, you see any wounds you have received beginning to heal miraculously — restore 10 VIGOUR points (up to the maximum limit of your *normal* VIGOUR score). You must now try one of the other substances — either the powder (turn to **90**) or the liquid (turn to **121**).

262

You hit the floor with a bone-jarring impact, but at least you are still alive. There is a thunderous crack and a burst of heat like an open furnace as the energy blast shoots over your head. The fraying tapestry shrivels away to expose the mirror beneath, and the full force of the bolt is reflected directly back at the creature itself! Its dying shriek goes on for a long time; you cover your ears to keep out the terrible noise.

When you look up, there is nothing left of your strange adversary apart from a charred and headless husk. The stench in the room is appalling, and you waste no time in staggering back into the next chamber. Minki pads quietly along beside you, perhaps sensing your shock at this brush with death.

Turn to **79**.

263

The steps descend only a few metres into a low tunnel. You can barely discern another set of steps in the shadows at the far end, this time leading up. As you walk along the tunnel, you pass a succession of sculpted faces that peer out from the walls. Even by the standards of Anku art they strike you as unnecessarily daunting, with features contorted into expressions of rage and terror, agony and wild delight. Each face has a gaping black maw — perhaps opening into deep recesses in the walls. If you wish to stop and investigate the carved faces more closely, turn to **147.** If you would rather carry straight on along the tunnel, turn to **214.**

264

You remember that the ruby dust bled from the stone serpents you fought. Perhaps it has magical properties. Your hunch is confirmed as soon as you cast the glittering dust out on to the steaming water. A sheet of translucent crystal, like hard crimson ice, forms rapidly. As the dragon surges through this, the crystal spreads up around its body. A sparkling shell encases the dragon and its struggles grow slower and more feeble as the shell hardens. At last it stops moving altogether, frozen forever in sinuous grace like a sculpture of solid ruby. You make your way past it along the line of rocks and leave the shaft through the arch in the north wall.

Turn to **156.**

Even in its damaged state, the golem is a powerful creature and will be hard to beat.

GOLEM   VIGOUR 9

Roll two dice:
score 2 to 6   You are hit; lose 4 VIGOUR
score 7 to 12   The golem loses 3 VIGOUR

If you win, turn to **14**. If you FLEE south along the gallery, turn to **72**.

The grille crashes to the dusty floor of the passage. You step through. As in the other passage, bas-reliefs form a warlike procession along the walls. The air is stale and dry, and you moisten your lips with a little water from your flask before going on. With Minki at your heels, you follow the passage west until you enter a large room where savage carvings merge with the walls and pillars.

Turn to **257**.

As you go on, the trees around you become less closely spaced and the ferns and bushes grow thicker and more luxuriant. Humming-birds whir and dart all around you, plundering nectar from the exotic flowers.

Before long the path forks again, and you can go left (turn to **173**) or right (turn to **44**).

268

As the first cadaver falls you see a chance to FLEE down the passage in the south wall. You may do so if you wish — but all three of the remaining cadavers will try to strike you as you FLEE, and you must make your AGILITY roll to avoid each. If you FLEE, turn to **15**. If not, the cadavers soon close the gap in their ranks and you must battle on.

Roll two dice:

score 2	You lose 9 VIGOUR
score 3 to 4	You lose 6 VIGOUR
score 5 to 7	You lose 3 VIGOUR
score 8 to 12	One of the cadavers loses 3 VIGOUR

If you defeat another, turn to **98**.

269

In the north wall of the corridor there is a side tunnel, at the end of which you can see a charred timber door. If you wish to walk down the tunnel and open the door, turn to **56**. If you would rather continue west, turn to **223**.

270

With energetic strides you mount the steps to the top of the pyramid. It is rather less tiring to ascend this smaller replica than it was to climb the full size version far above you! As you reach the top, you see a circular pit in the summit.

Suddenly a column of crimson light flares into life, descending from the high ceiling of the chamber down into the pit — and thence into the silver pyramid's heart. The only way on from here is to step into the beam of light…

You sheathe your sword, take a deep breath, and step off into space.

Turn to **176**.

271

The girl watches you with wild, scared eyes as you cut through the rope securing the cage and lower it gently to the ground. A single stroke of your knife chops through the twine holding the cage door shut.

She shrinks back and whimpers as you untie the silver wire, unable to understand your soothing words of reassurance. She cowers in a corner of the cage and makes no move towards freedom, so you leave the cage door open and continue on your way.

Turn to **209**.

272

The passage brings you to a large, high-ceilinged chamber. A torn silk robe lies at the entrance by your feet, seeming like a pool of black ink on the marble floor. When you stir it with the point of your sword a fine grey ash spills out. This tells you that it is the remains of one of Damontir's Nightmare Guard — silent, demonic assassins that crumble to dust when they are slain. Your enemy took this route into the temple labyrinth, then.

Minki hesitantly paws at a second, similar robe. You discover what killed them as you pass along to the far end of the chamber. Lying against the wall is the carcass of a huge clawed manticore – doubtless a guardian of the pyramid since time immemorial. The blood which flows from its many wounds is still sticky, still warm. Damontir and his retinue cannot be very far ahead of you. Cautiously you press on deeper into the labyrinth.

Turn to **122**.

273

Which item will you produce from your backpack:

A gilded sceptre?	Turn to **58**
A witchdoctor's wand?	Turn to **32**
A red gem?	Turn to **254**

If you do not think any of these will be of use, you must rely on your fighting skill (turn to **126**).

274

Damontir left two of his Nightmare Guard to ambush you. They prowl silently towards you from the darkness beyond the double doors. One holds a long bright icicle of a blade, the other's dagger is shorter and hooked like a vulture's beak. There is no room for you to dodge past them. If you are to pursue Damontir, you must first slay these shadowy assassins.

First NIGHTMARE GUARD   VIGOUR 12
Second NIGHTMARE GUARD   VIGOUR 12

Roll two dice:
score 2 to 4   You are hit twice; lose 6 VIGOUR
score 5 to 6   You are hit once; lose 3 VIGOUR
score 7 to 12   One of the Nightmare Guards (you
                     decide which) loses 3 VIGOUR

If you kill one of them, turn to **65**.

275

Even through the thick soles of your boots you can feel how hot the rocks are. As you cross them, you happen to dislodge a few loose pebbles which fall into the lake. You have not gone much further when the water nearby begins to churn and froth. There is an odd stinging odour as large murky bubbles break the surface. Suddenly a huge spout of water erupts into the air. As the fine, hot spray splashes all around you, you think at first that you are witnessing an underground geyser. But then you see something else: something red and gleaming rising up from the water. Two gold flecked eyes regard you with a look of reptilian spite. You stand in awe as the massive red dragon rears up and shakes the water from its burnished scales. Its wings span half the shaft. It watches you for a heart-stopping moment, steam hissing from its flared nostrils, then throws back its head and spreads wide its wings in a mighty intake of breath. Turn to **231**.

You roll the witchdoctor's body into the bushes and wipe his blood from your sword before pressing onwards. You are in low spirits, shamed by the murder you have committed. Minki rejoins you after a while, but he sterns to sense your gloom and slopes along at your heels with none of his former jollity. You wonder if the natives have found the witchdoctor's corpse yet. You can hear their groans and howls close behind you now, a score of voices joined in a threnody of vengeance. Realizing that you cannot outdistance them, you hastily camouflage yourself in a dense thicket. The natives run straight past your hiding place without spotting you. You listen to their war cries fading into the distance and you are confident that you have shaken them off. Just as you are about to disentangle yourself from the thicket and go on your way, Minki suddenly utters a strangled cry.

You look around. To your horror, your little companion is dead, a pool of blood is spreading from his twitching form. You start to rise, hand reaching for your sword, only to fall as an agonizing pain shoots up your leg. You think at first that a snake has attacked you, but when you see the thing clinging to your leg you know that the truth is infinitely more terrible. It is a shrunken head. More of the grisly creatures drop from the branches to sink their envenomed teeth into your flesh. Even from beyond the grave, the witchdoctor's spirit has guided these emissaries of retribution. You scream and scream, but to no avail. The shrunken heads feast, and in hours only your bones will remain.

The room beyond the antechamber is large and high-ceilinged. In the light of your magic sword you can just see a passage leading west out of the room. As you make your way over to this, you pass a line of pillars engraved with the stylized flame symbols of the god Katak. A massive block of polished red granite against the far wall may once have been an altar stone where heretics and prisoners of war would have met a grisly death. You are considering a detour to inspect the altar more closely, in case some magical relic is hidden inside it, when a figure steps from the shadows to face you. It stands upon two legs, but it is not human. Its skin is dark and thorny, it has cruel talons on two short reptilian limbs where its arms should be, and its 'head' comprises a single glowing orb of an eye on the end of a long stalk.

You are dumbstruck, bewildered; it is like no creature you have ever encountered. This hesitation almost costs you your life. As you falter, the creature discharges a searing beam of ruby light from its eye. At the same instant Minki leaps down from your shoulder, and this distracts the creature so that its energy blast goes slightly wide. Instead of hitting you it strikes the wall behind, vaporizing an ancient mural and causing the stone to blister and boil. The release of energy temporarily depletes the creature. Its eye burns a dull red now, but you can see it growing brighter by the second as the creature builds up for another shot. You could charge straight at it now, in the hope that you can reach it before it can fire another energy blast. If you wish to try that, turn to **48**. If you wish to try and escape from it, turn to **27**.

278

Despite the fierce psychic strain, you manage to throw off whatever spell the revenant attempted against you. It snaps its snaggle-toothed jaw in rage and closes to resume the battle.

Roll two dice:
score 2 to 6   You are wounded and lose 3 VIGOUR
score 7 to 12   The revenant loses 3 VIGOUR

If you win, turn to **110**.

279

The curse at last takes its delayed toll. You stagger as a dozen old wounds and battle scars reopen and bright blood drips down on to the floor around your feet. Roll two dice and add 3 to the total — this is how many VIGOUR points you lose before you can staunch the bleeding. If you are still alive, turn to **145**.

280

The native warriors snarl and posture threateningly, but they realize that any attempt to rush you would cost their witchdoctor his life. They feign blank incomprehension at first when you hold out your free hand towards the man who carries your sword. You tighten your grip on the witchdoctor's throat until his face is an awful shade of magenta, and your sword is then hastily returned to you. As the witchdoctor squirms and gurgles in your grasp, you look into the faces of the natives and see the naked hate in their eyes. You have the upper hand for the moment, but how will you keep them from coming after you when you leave the village? You consider several plans. Will you:

Set fire to their huts to keep them busy?	Turn to **105**
Take the witchdoctor with you as a hostage?	Turn to **299**
Force them all to get drunk on the brew in the witchdoctor's hut?	Turn to **233**

281

You reach out your hand… Turn to **259**.

282

It seems you cannot escape from the Malgash. Well, if that is so, you will show this fell demon the harsh price of hindering you in your quest!

THE MALGASH   VIGOUR 18 (unless you have already fought it and have reduced its VIGOUR)

Roll two dice:
| score 2 to 7 | You lose 4 VIGOUR |
| score 8 to 12 | The Malgash loses 3 VIGOUR; you lose 1 VIGOUR |

If you win, turn to **256.**

283

You deal the death-blow and the Simulacrum sinks back into the trembling quicksilver surface. Your reflection is clouded out as the surface swims with murky colours like a soap film. It breaks into shimmering bright nodules which drift outwards and gradually fade from view. A small mirror lies broken on the floor.

The battle has carried you back away from Damontir. As you turn to face him, he touches one of the runes on the podium and speaks a few guttural words in the extinct Anku tongue. Immediately there is a soft hiss and the high wall of flames that encloses you shrinks away. You stare in awe at the sheer immensity of the cavern, but the glint in Damontir's eyes is more purposefully directed.

Following his gaze, you look behind you. In an alcove like a fanged maw stands the gleaming golden idol of the flame-god. More than two thousand years have passed since any mortal last beheld it — last possessed it. The body is squat and powerful, each rippling muscle sculpted to perfection. The face shows the classical ideal of Anku nobility, though with the grotesque flourish of two serpentine tusks curving along the sharp high-boned cheeks. The eyes are huge faceted rubies.

You glance back to find Damontir watching you. His arm is raised towards you, and on his ungloved hand you see the Ring of Red Ruin. He was waiting for you to turn, so that you would see the look of gloating triumph. A tendril of crimson fire streaks towards your heart. You must be very quick to

dodge it. Roll two dice (or roll one die twice and add the scores together). If the total is less than or equal to your current AGILITY turn to **204**. If it is greater, turn to **13**.

284

The effect of the curse manifests itself at last. A number of old wounds and battle scars suddenly open, spilling your blood on the refulgent floor. Roll two dice and add 3 to the total — this is the number of VIGOUR points you lose. If you are still alive, turn to **60**.

285

Though one of your opponents falls, crumbling to dust like all of its kind when slain, the other fights on with no thought of retreat or surrender.

Roll two dice:

score 2 to 5	You are hit; lose 3 VIGOUR
score 6 to 12	The Nightmare Guard loses 3 VIGOUR

If you win, you continue northwards. Turn to **108**.

286

The revenant disintegrates and clatters in fragments to the stone floor. Its bony hands are still clinging to your tunic; it is only with considerable effort that you break their grip and hurl them away from you. You walk over to where Minki sits trembling. He whines and stares nervously into the shadows, but will not move. Eventually you pick him up and continue west.

Turn to **217**.

287

You try to evade the bolt but are too slow. Glowing plasma ignites your clothes, melts your armour and flesh, chars your naked bones. You are dead before you can draw breath to scream.

288

Three passages lead off from the end of the candlelit hall. From here, will you go east (turn to **116**), north (turn to **199**) or west (turn to **55**)?

289

In your panic you have become disorientated. You cannot see that you are staggering away from the pool. You strike the wall and collapse in a writhing heap. Your screams die to whimpers, and then only the echo of a whimper, as the inferno consumes you. Your quest has ended in failure and a horrible death.

290

You pause at an archway in the north wall of the corridor. A second corridor leads off beyond it. Will you head north along the new corridor (turn to **22**), or continue west (turn to **50**)?

291

You manage to grab the newel and stop yourself from falling. As you blunder on downwards, the dire spectres loom once more out of the darkness. Their faces are twisted in mad laughter now as they try to rip the soul from your body. If you score less than or equal to your current PSI on the total of two dice, turn to **139**. If you score higher than your PSI, turn to **247**.

292

You scramble along the tunnel. Bronze footsteps pound the flagstones behind you as the elemental lurches in pursuit. In return for its freedom, it offers only a swift and savage death. Once more, your breathing is shallow and painful, and now you guess the reason why. From the mouths of the graven faces seeps a heavy suffocating gas, ingeniously channelled along volcanic vents deep in the rock. But if the atmosphere in the tunnel will not sustain life, neither will it sustain the elemental. Its flame gutters and dies, and the armour falls in disjointed segments amid a clangorous noise like the pealing of a bronze bell. As you step back towards it, a wisp of smoke curls up from the visor and drifts down the tunnel. You watch it disperse and then hurry back to the room before the air in your lungs gives out. Turn to **135**.

293

You head gradually west through a succession of dusty rooms and narrow tunnels until you reach a corridor leading south. A short distance further on, this joins a second corridor running east and west. You decide to take the western branch. Turn to **190**.

294

Will you now leave by the tunnel in the north wall (turn to **146**), or will you go back the way you came (turn to **213**)?

295

The archway opens into an enclosed chamber from which steps lead down. Advancing with drawn sword to the top of the steps, you see a very long staircase leading right down into the bowels of the rock. Each step is inlaid with semi-precious stones; a tracery of gold lines adorns the walls. But Damontir ignored these treasures just as you do — you both know that the greatest prize, the idol of Katak, awaits you far below. You begin the steep descent. Every ten metres or so you come to a landing. The staircase continues to reach down into the darkness ahead of you. You are about halfway between the second and third landings when you tread upon a step which gives slightly under your weight. There is an ominous click, followed by a rumbling from the top of the stairs. You look back. A huge boulder, released from its hidden recess by the trap you have sprung, is rolling down the staircase towards you! As it thunders down, shaking the

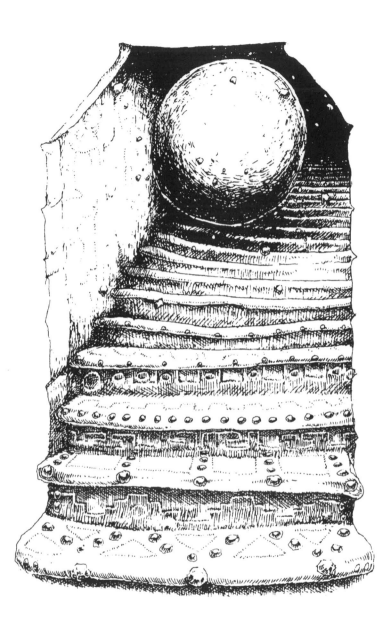

walls land causing dust to shower from the vaulted roof, you have no time to think — you must act now. Will you:

Fall flat where you are?	Turn to **46**
Run?	Turn to **175**
Lie flat on the steps just below the second landing?	Turn to **7**
Use your Ring of Intangibility (if you have one)?	Turn to **25**

296

As you approach the robe, a cobra rears up from within and uncoils towards you like a black lightning flash. You bring your sword down to slice the creature in two, but you are too slow to prevent it from sinking its fangs through the leather of your boot and deep into your flesh. As you cry out, the double doors beside you suddenly fly open.

You can quickly drink your snakebite antidote now, if you have any — it will neutralize the cobra's venom. Otherwise you must deduct 7 VIGOUR points.

If you are still alive, turn to **274**.

297

The poison that the scorpion pumped into you would kill most people. Pain contorts your muscles and a horrible darkness clouds the edge of your vision, but not for a second do you waver in your struggle for life.

Slowly — almost miraculously — you rise to your feet. At last, as you give vent to a groan of pain and defiance, you feel your strength returning. Although still trembling from the poison's residual effects (reduce all your Combat Rolls by 1 from now on), you are alive and able to carry on. You clamber up out of the pit and leave the room to make your way north.

Turn to **152**.

298

To your disappointment, the new passage leads to a dead end. You are about to retrace your steps when you happen to glance up and see a niche in the wall, slightly above head height. Standing on tiptoe, you see a pair of gold sandals. If you wish to take these and put them on, turn to **82**. If you decide to leave them where they are and return to the vestibule to head west, turn to **119**.

299

The natives watch as you back away and vanish into the jungle with their witchdoctor. You take his bone wand away so that he cannot employ any magic against you. He struggles with surprising vigour for one of his years, and you are careful to maintain a firm grip on him as you cut your way through the dense vegetation. Hunting cries break through the verdant gloom behind you — the natives are giving chase. Although they are some distance away, it will not take them long to catch up. Your hostage is slowing you down too much. Before continuing on your way, will you let him go (turn to **246**) or will you kill him (turn to **276**)?

300

At last, after so many years, you have had your revenge. Damontir sprawls lifeless at your feet. The body does not crumble to dust like one of the Nightmare Guard. Damontir was not a supernatural figure as some believed, then — just a twisted, noxious little man. With your fury spent, he hardly seems now to have been worth the killing.

You walk slowly over and stand before the idol. It is considerably larger than you had imagined, and since it must weigh close to two tonnes you are at a loss to know how to move it. Perhaps, after all, it is better to leave it here. Katak is a forgotten god whom history has passed by — to defile his memory by plundering the temple of its idol would be a churlish act, unworthy of a knight of Palados. You look into

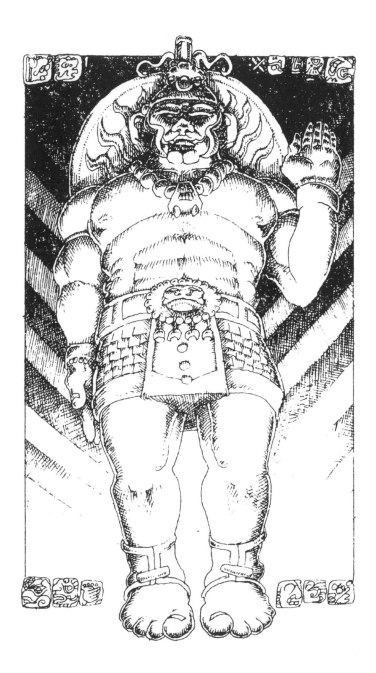

Katak's jewelled eyes and speak these sentiments aloud.

Suddenly you lose your balance and tumble into a whirlpool of colour and light. The idol and the cavern have vanished, but as you drift through a vortex of images you see the distant outline of your ship. As you watch, it leaps into focus. You seem to be plunging towards it. There is a sudden, brief burst of light and you find yourself standing on the creaking deck. The sailors are staring at you incredulously and the sight of their wide-eyed faces make you bellow with laughter. Your steward hurries forward and bows to you.

'My liege! We feared you had perished.' He looks up, as if to reassure himself that you are truly there. 'And now a great wonder has occurred for all to behold. A shaft of brilliant light descended from the top of yonder crystal spire, and when it faded you were standing here among us. And these items appeared also...'

You look where he is pointing. Behind you on the deck are a dozen large silver coffers. They are filled to overflowing with gems, medallions and artefacts of gold and other precious metals.

Still chuckling, you address your anxious steward, saying, 'Strange magic transported me here from the very bowels of the earth. The treasure is the gift of a god no longer worshipped.'

Perplexed, the old steward hobbles away to fetch wine and prepare your meal. You lean on the rail. The planking smells damp after the recent storm. The sun is close to setting, painting the sky with streaks of red and turning the dunnish river to molten gold. You look around to see a faint rainbow in the eastern sky.

'Prepare to set sail,' you tell the men. 'We're going home.'

If you enjoyed *The Temple of Flame*, try these other classic adventure gamebooks by Dave Morris…

It is the dawn of the 24th century and the Earth is dying. Gaia, a satellite array designed to repair the effects of global warming, is out of control. A new Ice Age tightens its inexorable grip on the planet. Humanity is on the edge of extinction.

Mankind's last hope is the Heart of Volent, a strange meteorite which has already brought mutation and chaos to the world. Legend says that the one who finds it shall wield the power to reshape the universe.

As the ice sheets spread and the world slides towards the brink, you and a handful of bitter rivals compete in the race for the Heart. Only one can win. Are you ruthless and resourceful enough to claim the ultimate prize?

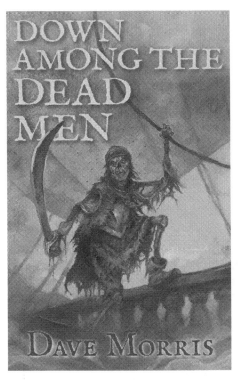

War is brewing between the kingdoms of Glorianne and Sidonia, a war waged for control of the territories of the New World. Galleons laden with gold ply the seas, and in their wake sail pirates and privateers eager for plunder.

Adrift in an open boat, you make your desperate bid to escape from the sadistic Captain Skarvench. You are determined to round up a crew, get yourself a ship, and set sail on a voyage of vengeance and justice. You are destined to face many perils: undead pirates, sea monsters, cursed ships, witches and ancient gods. And the greatest threat of all: the premonition of your own death at the hands of your hated foe.

DOWN AMONG THE DEAD MEN

The sole survivor of an expedition brings news of disaster. Your
twin brother is lost in the trackless western sierra. Resolving to
find out his fate, you leave the safety of your home far behind.
Your quest takes you to lost jungle cities, across mountains and
seas, and even into the depths of the underworld.

You will confront ghosts and gods, bargain for your life against
wily demons, find allies and enemies among both the living and
the dead. If you are brave enough to survive the dangers of the
spirit-haunted western desert, you must still confront the wizard
called Necklace of Skulls in a deadly contest whose stakes are
nothing less than your own soul.

NECKLACE OF SKULLS

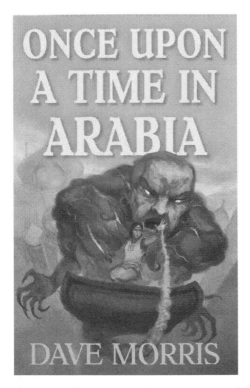

You have made a deadly enemy. Jafar, advisor to the Caliph, plans a coup that will put him on the throne of Baghdad. You are the only one who can warn the Caliph, but who will listen to a penniless adventurer? Especially as Jafar's assassins are scouring the city to find you.

You go in search of the fame and fortune that will give you the means to expose Jafar's treachery. Your travels take you to ghoul-haunted oases, magical palaces, lost cities of gold, and uncharted isles full of mystery and danger. Threatened by bandits, fire wizards, thieves and fearsome creatures, you must risk all in your determined quest to save the kingdom.

ONCE UPON A TIME IN ARABIA

FABLED LANDS

A sweeping fantasy role-playing campaign in gamebook form

Set out on a journey of unlimited adventure!

FABLED LANDS is an epic interactive gamebook series with the scope of a massively multiplayer game world. You can choose to be an explorer, merchant, priest, scholar or soldier of fortune. You can buy a ship or a townhouse, join a temple, undertake desperate adventures in the wilderness or embroil yourself in court intrigues and the sudden violence of city backstreets. You can undertake missions that will earn you allies and enemies, or you can remain a free agent. With thousands of numbered sections to explore, the choices are all yours.